BEFORE FIVE IN A ROW

BY

JANE CLAIRE LAMBERT

Before Five in a Row

ISBN 1-888659-04-1

Published by:
Five in a Row Publishing
P.O. Box 707
Grandview, MO, 64030-0707
(816) 246-9252

Send all requests for information to the above address.

Original cover oil painting created for *Five in a Row* by:
Deborah Deonigi
P.O. Box 1140
Maple Valley, WA 98038
(206) 413-9118

To Carolyn...
A wonderful mother,
a teacher's teacher,
and my friend.

 # Table of Contents

Making the Most of *Before Five in a Row*

What delights a young child? There are many things, but for most children having someone read him a book is near the top of the list. To luxuriate in the security of a person who will give a child his time, allowing the child to snuggle as close as he wants, and share with him a wonderful story is one of the highlights of childhood! Sometimes a child wants the same story read over and over again. Because the stories are simple ones, this repetition may become tiring for the reader. So, *Before Five in a Row* suggests a wide variety of interesting topics and activities to present, now and then, after a story is read. These discussions and activities provide added interest for both the *reader* and the child.

The stories included in this volume are wonderful stories for early childhood. Because many of them are classics and because they are *good*, you, along with your older children, may find yourselves appreciating them, too. But, this series of "little lessons" was created especially to bring enjoyment to children ages two through four. The point is not so much to *instruct* or *teach* as it is to have a happy introduction to books, provide an interesting, light introduction to many different topics, and to build intimacy between the reader and child. The topical subject headings are only to *suggest* in what areas these activities might *lay a foundation* for academic subjects to be encountered by your child in later grades.

Remember that two-year-olds cover a vast range of differing abilities. Some two-year-olds will not yet be able to sit still through an entire story, let alone answer questions or discuss it. They may not want to hunt for items in the illustrations. That's perfectly normal. There are many other ideas in Part Two, The Parent's Treasury of Ideas, that you can make use of now and save Part One, The *Story* Section, for six months or a year. You can't do all of these ideas at once anyway. If you are patient, there will come a day when your child delights in the "story activities," and in the meantime you will have had lots of fun playing together.

Many of the stories used in *Before Five in a Row* are simple. Some have less detail than other picture books in terms of setting or illustration, etc. Yet each of them has a special warmth and charm that keeps your child wanting to experience them over and over. Several of the stories included have repetitious wording. A young child finds it challenging to be able to tell a story before it's finished. Repetition helps him learn and remember the story so he knows it well enough to beat you to the punch line. In addition, rereading the story several times allows you to make different comments at each reading. Keep your teaching subtle and your child will enjoy both the stories and the related activities you share together.

For each story title chosen for *Before Five in a Row* you will find suggested activities. These activities can follow the reading of the stories. Many times you will read a story and not do *any* activity directly following it. Other times you will decide to bring up a topic and talk it over together. You might choose to read one of the stories during the day and save a question or discussion for lunch or dinner time. You could say, "Remember when we read about the little girl on the bus? What other ways are there to get from one place to another?" You can even bring up activities or questions from previously read stories when you are on a walk together, standing in line at the supermarket, or during bath time, etc. *Anytime* is a good time to share the stories and activities that build a warm closeness between a parent and child.

You will undoubtedly read many other stories not included in *Before Five in a Row*. There are wonderful Richard Scarry stories, the beloved books of Dr. Seuss, Beatrix Potter and many, many more waiting to be discovered and read. But, when you want a special story with "ready to use" activities and ideas that inspire creative interaction, pick up a *Before Five in a Row* story and enjoy!

The subject heading listed at each story activity shows how the ideas in *Before Five in a Row* lay the foundation for *future* formal academic training in each of these subject areas. *Before Five in a Row* is *not* attempting to teach academics, but rather to provide a strong foundation of academic "readiness". Resist the temptation to try to create two-year-old professors to be proud of. In the long run, pushing toddlers to leap tall academic buildings in a single bound does *not* produce the

results most parents want. Metaphorically speaking, it's like trying to teach a child to walk before he's mastered scooting, rolling and crawling! Some children might be able to learn academic material at a very early age, but vital maturity steps have been skipped in the rush.

Above all, the time between ages two and four should be a time of sharing, hugging, reading, singing, dancing, puzzles, blocks, outdoor excursions, swinging high, playing in the sand box and enjoying fascinating introductions to the wonderful world of life.

The ideas presented in *Before Five in a Row* are not meant to teach in depth, but only to enhance your child's awareness of the world around him and create memorable times of interaction between you. So, don't take the academic titles too seriously. They are only provided to show *you* what areas of future learning you'll be developing. Also, a short Bible verse has been included for each lesson plan, if you care to use it.

Besides the *Before Five in a Row* stories and activities, make sure that you include many different kinds of play with your child. Enjoy games like Ring Around the Rosy, London Bridge Is Falling Down, and Hide and Seek. There are also the finger-play hand games. Perhaps you remember, "This is the church, this is the steeple, open the doors and see all the people," from your own childhood. Have fun making creative use of puppets and puppet plays. (Puppets don't need to be expensive. Simple homemade puppets delight children at this age.) Take time to enjoy the wonders of nature together. Whether gazing at the stars or watching an industrious ant or bee, it is good to appreciate God's creation. Spend lots of time together searching for exciting examples of beauty and wonder.

Remember, too, that activities in which you take the time to include your child, such as going to a children's play, short music or dance programs, or even trips to certain interesting stores all help to broaden his experience of life. He becomes more aware and pleasantly excited about the world around him, stimulating his natural curiosity and desire to know more. This desire to learn is the foundation you want firmly in place *long before* you begin his formal academic training. When a child is excited and curious, he *wants* to learn! To help you recall many activities that you might have played once but forgotten, there is a Parent's Treasury of Creative Ideas for Learning Readiness beginning on page 105, which contains many additional ideas and projects for ages two through four.

Someday, when our children are grown, very few of us will say, "I sure wish I had sold more at my job, or won more awards at work, or opened more new accounts for my employer." But many of us may say, "I wish I had spent more time with my children when they were young."

It is a *very* brief window of time, but a solid foundation during these early years can make a lifetime of difference for you *and* your child. Enjoy some of the ideas in *Before Five in a Row* and make the most of these precious years!

Part One

Before Five in a Row
Stories and Activities

Here are some quick special memory makers. They only require a parent or an older sibling to read a story to a young child and then choose a topic to explore together. Or if you choose an activity from Part Two, *The Parent's Treasury of Ideas*, the only requirement is a parent or older sibling that wants to have fun and play together.

JESSE BEAR, WHAT WILL YOU WEAR?

Title: *Jesse Bear, What Will You Wear?*
Author: Nancy White Carlstrom
Illustrator: Bruce Degen
Copyright: 1986
Award: Jr. Literary Guild Selection

Summary

Jesse Bear is excited about his clothing for the day and irresistibly draws the reader right into the experience. A delightfully rousing romp in rhyme!

Bible

A cheerful heart makes good medicine (Proverbs 17:22) and a happy heart makes a cheerful face (Proverbs 15:13). (Repeat often in a cheerful way!)

Language Arts

Nancy White Carlstrom has written glorious, joyous rhyme! Enjoy it over and over. Wake your child up in the morning with a smile on your face and the words of this poem. These words and rhythms teach young ears to appreciate our language and the sounds it can make. *What Will You Wear, Jesse Bear?* provides the kind of verse that lays a foundation for appreciation of poetry in later years. These are the rhymes of early childhood!

Loving Relationships

On a subsequent reading, ask your child if he'd like to look for signs of love between Jesse Bear and his parents. There is a page where Father Bear hugs and kisses Jesse. There is the greeting when Father Bear comes home from work. And, there is a picture where Father Bear has been reading the newspaper but looks up eager and interested as Mother Bear and Jesse decide what Jesse should wear at night. Mother Bear shows her affection for Jesse by kindly helping him in the morning (front cover) and in her loving watchfulness on the first page of text. She continues her kind care and finishes by blowing him a kiss as she turns off the light. Enjoy these scenes together and create many such daily scenes and traditions (special waking, mealtime, naptime and bedtime traditions) of your own. They make wonderful memories.

Colors, Patterns, and Combinations

As a prelude to learning to choose clothes to wear, have a box with many different colors of cloth swatches, possibly five or six inches square. Include different colors, patterns and even textures. Let your child spread several out and look at them and then see if he enjoys putting them together like outfits. (His choices might sometimes seem outrageous to you, but now is not the time to criticize. Just let him enjoy the possibilities.) Make a cardboard "bear body." Use it to give him the idea of one color swatch for a top and another for a bottom combination. If you like, cut the color swatches to fit like shirts and shorts. You might have him pick a matching outfit, where the top and the shorts are from the same cloth. Then ask him to choose another outfit where the top and bottom are of different color combinations. This could lead to his observing people and the clothing combinations *they* wear. The world is full of variety to be observed and appreciated. Maybe he'll tell you when someone

is wearing something he thinks looks attractive. Another way to learn about color and pleasing combinations is to become a nature watcher. For instance, the red and green of a hummingbird is lovely. Spring showcases purples and yellows and greens, while fall's palette becomes reds, golds, oranges and browns. The luscious greens, browns, blues and oranges of shellfish are magnificent. Watch how the Lord has created using color. Point out new discoveries to each other and be amazed! It might be fun to get a large book on shells, butterflies, insects or rocks, etc. (photographed or paintings), from the library and just *look* at it with your child in a quiet moment. You do not need to tell him what everything is or try to "teach" him, but rather just appreciate the immense variety and color of creation. Remark on the pictures that you particularly like and listen to your child as he points out his favorites. Remember the Robert Louis Stevenson verse: *The world is so full of a number of things, I'm sure we should all be as happy as kings!*

Fine Arts - Drama

(Use this activity *after* you've read the story several times.) Parents or older siblings can make up a pantomime to the words of *Jesse Bear*. While one person reads the text, another uses pantomime to portray the actions that Jesse Bear made. If you can imagine "Dad stuck in the chair at noon" or with "sand on his hand" (pretending to be playing in a sandbox), you might be able to imagine how your young child would love this. Get ready for possible giggles of delight! No one activity is guaranteed to delight a child. If he doesn't like this one, try another. Great family memories are worth pursuing.

Literature

Nancy White Carlstrom has written *Jesse Bear* asking what he will wear in the morning. Eloise Wilkin has also written a "morning" book that you might enjoy reading. It is called *My Good Morning Book*, 1984 Golden Press, ISBN 0307122719. It is published in the hard cardboard young child's format and has beautiful pictures. *My Good Morning Book* makes a pleasant beginning to any day!

Poetry and Art

"*Jesse Bear* Continued" This is an easy rhyme *pattern* to continue. Perhaps you or an older sibling would enjoy composing additional verses to the *Jesse Bear* poem. These verses could center around various events which Jesse might encounter in any given day. What might Jesse wear on a rainy day or a snowy day? What might he wear to a birthday party or the beach? A rhyme for a snowy day "after the manner of Nancy Carlstrom" might be:

Jesse Bear, What will you wear?
It's snowing outside this morning.

My new snow suit
My mittens and boots
For this snowy, blowy morning!

Or how about a rainy day verse?

Jesse Bear, What will you wear?
It's storming outside this morning!

My slicker and hat
With the boots that match
Keep me dryer than dry
In the morning.

Now, for any new verses you make up, create a Jesse Bear cardboard, paper-doll and new clothes to match the story. For instance, he might wear a shirt and tie to a birthday party, etc. If you enjoy this, make the clothes for Nancy Carlstrom's story scenes, too. Then your child will be able to dress his Jesse Bear as you read the story! (Of course, if you are a tailor or seamstress and your child has a bear similar to Jesse Bear, you could surprise and delight him every now and then with a new sewn outfit, to go with the story or for new verses which you've created.)

"Can You Find" Searches

The wonderful illustrations by Bruce Degen make a good "searching field." On one reading of the story you might have your child look for all the bears he can see in the pictures. Let him point them out to you as you read. There are bears in the chubby crunchy cereal on the dedication page. There is also a bear face on the bib, pajamas, the towel rack, and the high chair. Find a bear clock, cookie cutter, and cookie jar, as well as a bear in the newspaper and the helicopter on the toy shelf. Also locate the bear slippers, a bear angel on the bed, and a bear spaceman lamp!

As you read the story another time, ask your child if he'd like to search for the pages that show flowers. There are many different kinds of flowers on various pages. Do you have some of these flowers in your garden? Show them to your child and let him smell the roses! (Make sure you scoot the bees away first.) If you do not grow flowers, go for a walk and point out some lovely gardens in which he can take delight. Another reading could begin a search for pictures that show food. After reading and finding the food pictures, ask your child what food pictured is his favorite.

Recognizing patterns

If you have an American flag handy, show it to your child and talk about the colors—red, white and blue, and the shapes—stripes, rectangles, and stars. Sing a song like "Yankee Doodle" or "America, the Beautiful" and let him wave the flag. Now, read the story of *Jesse Bear* and if he doesn't mention it, eventually draw his attention to the ball. It is shown on the cover, the first page of text and then on the toy shelf in two separate pictures. Does it remind him of the American flag? Why? Talk about the similarity of colors and shapes. Maybe in the future he will notice similar flag-like patterns in clothing and store items.

Order

Did your child notice, or make any comment on Jesse Bear's neat drawers full of clothes or the fact that at night when he went to bed the toys were mostly on the shelves? It is never too early to gently help a child learn that a basically orderly life flows more smoothly with much less frus-

tration and wasted time. Your very young child doesn't need to have a *full* understanding right now of how helpful this lifestyle might be. Just mentioning that Jesse Bear seems to care about his room, etc., might inspire interest in keeping things neat and in order. Sometimes when you see your child put something away (even if you've asked him), you could say, "My, but you keep your things in an orderly way, just like Jesse Bear!"

Look at the picture on the page following the last page of text. It is the picture of a clothes hamper with some clothes hanging out. Does your child have a special place where he can put his clothes? There are clothes bags, clothes hampers, laundry chutes, and other systems of laundry care. If he doesn't have a special place, create one for him. Sew up a large bag with a drawstring at the top. Then appliqué a face like Jesse Bear's on it! Or paint it on with puff paints.

Also, ask your child what is in the clothes hamper at Jesse Bear's house. The picture shows a "red something" and a "blue-striped something." Does your child know what these items are? The red shirt is the one that was "covered with dirt" and the blue striped items are Jesse Bear's pajamas with the boat on the front. Look for these pajamas. They are pictured on the title page and the picture opposite the title page, as well as in the picture opposite the first page of text. (If you can find or make them, your young child might enjoy having blue-striped pajamas like Jesse Bear's!)

Details

After reading Jesse Bear one day, turn to the page where he is in bed asleep. Have fun pointing out the details and searching for: the spaceman lamp, the globe, the piggy bank, the blocks, the ball, the boat, the rubber duck, the teddy bear, etc. Then mention the flowered rug, windows, wallpaper, dressers and shelves, etc. How many of these things does your child have in *his* room? (A basement room might not have windows, but rugs and shelves, a ball, blocks, etc., while another room might not have a rug, or a globe, but has wallpaper and dressers. What does your child's room have?)

Look with your child at the bathtub scene. Can he think of any reason that Jesse's parents chose to decorate the bathroom with swans? It seems to tie in to the "things in water" theme and be more appropriate than a circus, for instance. (Although, on second thought, at age three a child might dearly love to take baths while watching an active circus on the wall!) Sometime when your child is taking a bath, remind him of the "swans swimming" picture in *Jesse Bear* and have fun thinking together of all the things that could be found in the water such as ducks, fish, whales, boats, beach balls, etc. Watch out! It might be a long list.

Games to Play

Jesse Bear says he has a blanket that's blue and he plays peek-a-boo. There are many games like peek-a-boo that bring delight and giggles to a young child. Some others might be Pat-a-Cake, Ring Around the Rosy, London Bridge Is Falling Down, and Pop-Goes-the-Weasel. If you want more ideas, see your library for books. Or you can buy the Wee Sing tape, *Wee Sing Children's Songs and Fingerplays*, ISBN 0843137932.

Science

Jesse Bear enjoys the thought of stars overhead and moonlight streaming through his window. Find the right time, and in a darkened room, take your young child to the window and point out the moon. (When a full moon is low in the eastern sky it often looks large and yellow.) From time to time, draw your child's attention to the all the wonders of the sky. Your child's amazement and appreciation will grow like Jesse Bear's.

Jesse Bear also likes to see the flowers and chase the butterflies. Find butterflies in a familiar field and enjoy just running after them. Great exercise! If there is a flower garden near, you can often see a butterfly close-up sipping nectar from a flower. (Do keep an eye out for bees!)

Shapes

There is an illustration in *Jesse Bear* that shows a kitchen floor with carpet or linoleum covered with shapes. Find the circles, squares and triangles in the picture. Then make some potato stamps in these shapes and get different colors of paints or stamp pads and some large pieces of paper. Let your child make a design of his own.

YELLOW BALL

Title: *Yellow Ball*
Author: Molly Bang
Illustrator: Molly Bang
Copyright: 1991

Summary

Play ball! Then watch what happens in this sea adventure.

Bible

The yellow ball is caught up by the waves and floats out to sea, weathers a storm, and comes safely back again. After a few readings of this story, remind your child of the incident in Luke 8:22-25. In this story, Jesus is in a boat on a large lake. A storm comes up and Jesus calms the wind and the water. His boat makes it safely to the other side of the lake. You can recount these verses by saying, "The story *Yellow Ball* reminds me of something that happened to Jesus. He, too, was out on the waters, and went through a storm. He calmed the wind and the waves and arrived safely on the other side of the lake."

Art

With paint or construction paper let your child interpret or reproduce the picture on the title page—lighter blue sky above, a big yellow circle and darker blue-green below. First, let your child look at the picture. Talk about the colors you see in the illustration and *then* give him paint, crayons or colored paper and let him make what he sees in the picture!

Playing Ball

One day after reading the story with your child, bring out a surprise new ball. It would be fun if you could find a yellow one! How many different games can you play with the ball? There is catch, of course, and rolling it on the floor to each other while you are both sitting. Then you can hide the ball and see if the other one can find it. If you are outside, your child could throw the ball to you while his back is turned toward you (throwing it to you, over his head or between his legs). You can hit the ball with large plastic bats or brooms as if playing golf or hockey.

Enjoy the details of the copyright and dedication page with your child. Have you ever taken him on a picnic? Has he gone with someone else? Has he ever been to a lake or ocean beach? Does he think it looks like fun? Make a list of all the beach things you see: sunglasses, beach balls, sand pails, colorful beach towels, sandals, beach umbrellas, beach chairs, toy boats, coolers, bathing suits, inner tubes, etc.

Pastels

Pastel (a type of chalk) was used for some of the illustrations (others are of tempera). Look again at the pastel drawings of the copyright and dedication page. Notice the shaggy lines that look a little like crayon? Look at the blue plaid blanket on the copyright page. If you look closely you can see that the orangey color was applied over the blue square—one of the advantages of the pastel medium. Also, why do you think blue was chosen for the end papers at the front and back of this story? **Warning: Many Pastels Are Toxic! Be careful to select non-toxic art materials for your young child.**

After a reading, turn to the copyright and dedication page and look for as many different colored balls as you can find. There are red, green, blue, yellow, and orange balls, etc., on these two pages.

Follow the Ball

As you read the story, assure your child that the yellow ball appears in *every* picture. Sometimes it is hard to find. Let him search, and if there are some pictures where he cannot find it, save them for him to find on another reading. Eventually he will be able to see the ball in each picture as it travels out to sea and back again.

At another reading, you could talk about how the ball looks large in some pictures and very small in others. That might be enough discussion for now, or you could begin to explore the reason for this perception. Why does the ball look small in this picture but large in another? Why does your child think this is so? If he is ready to understand, explain that objects can appear large or small based on the distance from which they are viewed. Show how this is so in the pictures. You can hold a ball right in front of a your child's face and look how *big* it appears. Now walk to the other end of the room and look how *small* the ball appears. If it's a nice day you can set the ball down and walk several hundred feet away. *Now* how does the ball look? Use outings with your child to look for examples of this phenomenon.

When you've read the story again, locate the page where the ball begins to drift away and the text reads, "Uh-oh." Name as many actions as you can identify on this page. One man is floating, while many swim, some dive (you can only see *their* feet!), and some are carried. You can see the action of kicking feet in the water and sometimes only heads are visible, meaning that the people either have their feet on the bottom or are treading water.

Has your child ever viewed a fish from underneath? If you have an aquarium or fish bowl or if you visit a large public aquarium, try to get a view of the fish from *beneath*. A view of the fish from *above* seems almost as odd. Artists usually illustrate fish from the side view, giving us a profile. Watch for illustrations of fish in books, magazines and in works of art. (Can you imagine? Ten years from now, your child might see an unusual picture of a fish and remember when you read *The Yellow Ball* and first began to look for pictures of fish! Reading and discussing together certainly builds intimacy!)

Science

Storms are a regular part of life at sea. If you live in an area where there are storms you might, after a reading of this story, discuss the progress of a storm. First the wind picks up. Then it blows hard as the waves begin to rise. Rain follows, usually with lightning. Eventually the storm moves on. Often, objects are washed up on the beach during a storm. Shells, driftwood and other items are found on a beach after a storm has passed.

Science

Moonlight on Quiet Water. After a reading of the story, turn to the page that says, "Quiet now," and have your child look at the full illustration on both pages. There seem to be *two* balls in the picture. Ask your child about this. Does he realize that the ball on the *left* page is really the moon? It might be a yellow ball too! There is a broken white line on the left hand page beneath the moon. Point this out and ask what it might be. Maybe your child will know it is the reflection of moonlight on the water. Even though there is not much color in this two-page illustration, the smooth waves definitely give a feeling of peace after the wild action of the previous pages. (Notice, too, the tremendous contrast of color between this "quiet wave" dark page and the beautiful colors of the next illustration.)

Sequencing

Look at the illustrations above the words *look* and *hug*. These three pictures occur in a sequence. What happens first? (The child sees something yellow a long way ahead of him.) What happens next? (The child looks at the ball and reaches for it.) What happens then? (The child hugs it to him and smiles a big smile.) Reading stories together should be fun. Don't overdo the accompanying activities when you read with your child. But now and then, after a reading of a story, it is good to ask your child questions that illustrate patterns or sequences of events, such as "What happened first?" "Next," etc.

MY BLUE BOAT

Title: *My Blue Boat*
Author: Chris L.Demarest
Illustrator: Chris L. Demarest
Copyright: 1995

Summary

Follow a sailboat out to sea and home to port in an exhilaratingly illustrated picture book. You can taste the salt spray!

Bible

My Blue Boat sailed out on the sea and saw many things. Whales and dolphins and storms and stars all held a wonder for the little boat and its occupant. Psalm 107:23-24 tells about those who go to the sea in ships and who see the wonderful works of the Lord!

Parent's Note

This book covers the same theme as *Yellow Ball*, by Molly Bang. However, in this case it is a toy *boat* rather than a ball that goes to sea and returns. Normally, we would not use two books so similar and yet each one seemed too special to omit. Therefore, we have included this title with a few suggested activities and hope that you will treasure both of these stories. Enjoy comparing and contrasting the two books, while dreaming of the sea!

Art: Medium

These two books are illustrated with different media. The pictures in *Yellow Ball* are pastels (crayon-like chalks) and tempera, while the illustrations in *My Blue Boat* are watercolor and India ink. You do not necessarily need to mention this to your child. He'll enjoy just looking at the wonderful illustrations.

You may wish to help him with some preliminary experimentation in watercolor. Then, he might notice the similarity of his experiments to the illustrations of *My Blue Boat*. (Try taking a white paper plate and brushing a few strokes of rich blue watercolor across it. Then let your child drip a few drops of water off his brush onto the plate. Let him see how the color spreads out and runs. Show him similar areas in the watercolor illustrations of Demarest. A good example is the picture on the pages with the text, "and steer through storms". The paint splotches look as if raindrops had fallen on the page!)

Art: Color

The title of this story contains the name of a color. In fact, the title speaks of a *blue* boat. After enjoying the story together, you could remind your child of the book by Molly Bang about the ball that drifted out to sea. Ask him what color is included in the title of *that* story. (The title is *Yellow Ball*.)

Can your child match on paper some of the colors of *My Blue Boat* with his box of paints? Or perhaps he might name them.

Language: Vocabulary

My Blue Boat is rich in new vocabulary words. You do not need to explain every new word in one reading. But, over many, many readings you will have a chance to introduce the meaning of words like: channel, harbor, fleet, swells, whales, dol- phins, steer, drift, and beacon—all found in the text. Even if you do not explain all of these words, your child will like the sound of them. When he is older, he will recognize these words as he meets them again, and he will be ready to comprehend their meanings. (If you look at the illustrations, you could also include the words dock, lighthouse, oars, tugboat, and ferry.) But remember, at this age learning should be a by-product with the enjoyment of *reading together* the main goal. Work with *your child's* interest. Keep it fun!

Tracking

One day after reading the story, go back to the title page and let your young child point to the blue boat. Then have him point to and track the blue boat as you quickly turn the pages. Don't forget, there is one last blue boat on the outside back cover of the book!

Another day, use your finger to trace each line of boats on the inside of the book cover pages. When you get to the end of the line, go back to the beginning of the next line and trace across *again* until you reach the bottom of the page. (There are six lines of boats.) Maybe your young child will want to copy your actions. This tracking left to right is actually an important reading readiness skill that he will just be playing as a game!

Art and Action

The page where the blue boat dances with the whales is reminiscent of a Van Gogh painting in action and brush-stroke. Have on hand a book or reprint of *Starry Night* and other Van Gogh paintings that you think appropriate and that remind you of Demarest's story picture. Enjoy both artists' work.

There is a lot of action in this painting as the whales move about in the water. If you have access to a pool for swimming (and it's the right season), pretend you are dancing whales in the water. Make big splashes and turn in circles. If you have several members of your family or friends along, have someone pretend they are the blue boat moving among the sea creatures. (If you cannot use a pool, your child can pretend he is a whale splashing and turning in circles even in a wading pool, or a bath tub if you don't mind the mess! Actually, you can act out this whole scene in the living room or the backyard. Just *pretend* you're in the water!)

Science

After an enjoyable reading of the story, you might want to bring up the subject of whales and dolphins. There are some great bathtub toys of whales and dolphins. You could surprise your child with one of these. If he becomes interested in the subject, you can find simple books that tell about these water animals. If you have a marine aquarium near you that has a whale or dolphin exhibition, think about visiting with your child.

Imagine yourself as a young three-year-old, having read *My Blue Boat*, and having seen simple books about whales, and then actually seeing one! There is nothing to compare with that kind of excitement.

Comparison

There are many pictures in *My Blue Boat* that have a counterpart picture in the book, *Yellow Ball* by Molly Bang. With your child, look at both stories and find pictures that show the same theme of a passing town, wide sea, storms, a sleeping child in bed, etc. Can you find more?

Boats

After reading the story, try making a simple boat. It can be fashioned from paper, wood or aluminum foil. It may or may not have a sail. Your child's boat might be a special wooden creation built by Dad or an older sibling. He can sail it in the tub, in a wading pool, or at a small stream. Just like Chris Demarest in *My Blue Boat*, encourage your child to make up a story about *his* boat, where it goes and what it sees along the way. Remember to write down the boat's adventure. Boats usually have names. Ask him if he'd like to name his boat.

As he sails, maybe he will discover that in order to get much movement for his boat he needs wind in a sail, or water flowing along as in a stream. (An attached string or fishing line will allow a toy boat to sail down a creek or rivulet as your child follows along, without the danger of the boat getting away.) You could even call your child "captain" or "skipper!" Have fun! If your child becomes interested in this subject, here are two other books he might enjoy: *Sailor Dog*, by Margaret Wise Brown, 1992, Golden Press, ISBN 0307158152, and *Scuffy the Tugboat*, Little Golden Book.

Science: Stars

The occupant of the blue boat looks for stars in the night sky. You might ask your child if he thinks the stars look different out on the open sea. He may not have a reply to this question, but let him think for a moment. Then, if you need to, explain that there are no lights, like street lights and lights from cars or buildings out on the sea. When it is *really* dark you can see the stars and see more of them than you can in a town or city. This is something to just briefly mention—a thought for your child to ponder. He will be learning more about stars in years to come. (An extremely observant child might mention that one source of light near the seacoast is a lighthouse. But, in general, star watching is more magnificent when you are out at sea rather than in a city.) You can enhance your view of the stars by driving out into the country, away from city lights!

THE LITTLE RABBIT

Title: *The Little Rabbit*
Author: Judy Dunn
Photographs: Phoebe Dunn
Copyright: 1980

Summary:
Sarah and her friends find that pets are great!

Bible
Sarah takes good care of her little rabbit Buttercup and of Buttercup's babies. The Bible says that a wise man is kind to his animals, Proverbs 12:10a.

Illustrations
This book is different from any other *Before Five in a Row* title. The difference is in the illustrations which are *photographs* rather than draw-ings or paintings. Let your child look at this book next to Beatrix Potter's illustrations for *The Tale of Peter Rabbit* or Margaret Wise Brown's *Run Away Bunny*, etc. Enjoy the pictures of each book and if you like, mention that *The Little Rabbit* has photographs of a *real* rabbit. Show your child photographs of himself and talk about how you take them with a camera. This photographic art is different from the drawings and paintings of the other rabbit titles. Look for more photographs of rabbits in books and magazines and point them out to him.

Colors
After reading the story, look at the photograph with the bright pink clover and Sarah's yellow shirt. Then take a big box of either 48 or 72 crayons. (This box should be kept specifically for this type of exercise—they are not fat enough for your youngest child to use easily, yet.) Let your child pick from this assortment of colors one that

he thinks matches Sarah's shirt or the clover or Buttercup's pale pink ears. If he enjoys this exercise, let him try to match the purple of Sarah's backpack, her blue shirt or jumper and the brown of the basket. Matching is usually fun and a great way to increase color *awareness*. You and your child might share with each other your favorite shades of color. Keep looking for interesting new colors in nature, in clothes and in home designs.

Science

Sarah's bunny is white. Other domestic bunnies are black and some are different shades of brown. But, the wild bunny is "wild bunny brown." Show your child the photographs of the white bunny and the wild bunny. Compare them. Which is easier to see? Why might the wild bunny be brown? Camouflage is a big word! But, if you make it a game and *dramatically* say the word and explain it, you will probably get a laugh. At the same time you will have built the groundwork for future science understanding. Wild rabbits have many predators and their coloring is meant to be a partial means of protection. In places where there is a lot of snow, some rabbits' winter coats even turn white!

Science: Eyes and Ears

Some day after reading the story, take a trip to a pet store, farmer's market or an actual farm to see a real rabbit. Perhaps your neighbor has a pet rabbit. Once you find a real rabbit to examine, ask your child where the rabbit's eyes are. They are on the *sides* of its head and rather far back.

This means that a rabbit sees better to each side and even slightly behind him than he can see straight ahead. Most birds, except for owls, also have eyes that are more on the sides of their heads. Now, what about those ears! If it is an adult rabbit, your child will see large ears that turn to catch sounds in every direction. If this rabbit investigation is enjoyable, continue by looking at the big teeth for biting and the big legs for running.

Toys and Stories

One way to make a story an extra special experience is to make or purchase a stuffed animal that closely resembles the animal in the book. Keep it a surprise and bring it out after a few readings. You might want to introduce the new toy to your child by naming it after the book's character. Because the animal has the same name as the book character, the toy will be a reminder of special times of reading together and playing with the story character for years to come.

Pets

If you have the resources, time and ability to care for an animal, connecting a *real* pet to a story provides an unforgettable memory. Having a pet demonstrates to your child the importance of caring for creatures, showing them love and kindness. Even your young child watching *you* feed and care for a pet daily, begins to understand the importance of disciplined responsibility. You are the model after which he will pattern himself when he is older. This follows the basic training steps of observation and imitation.

If you are able to have a pet, then naming the pet becomes a special part of the process. What did Sarah call her rabbit? What did she name the babies and how did she think of those names? (Because there were seven bunnies, Sarah decided to name them for the days of the week.) Find at your library and enjoy *The Best of Friends: Classic Illustrations of Children and Animals*, compiled by Pamela Prince. Be sure to read the introduction for a discussion of the many benefits a child derives from having a pet! Beautiful book!

Animal Babies

In this story, you are able to watch tiny baby bunnies and how they grow. In the first place, Sarah has to wait a long time for Buttercup's bunnies to be born. Rabbits have about a thirty day gestation period. In the wild, they seldom live more than a year, so they reproduce rapidly with several litters in each season. But, pet rabbits often live five years or more. Talk about how Sarah has to wait a long time for the bunnies to arrive. You can help your child get a better grasp of how long a month is by reminding them of something special that happened a month ago. While that may seem like only "yesterday" to you—it will seem like *forever* to your young child!

When bunnies (and kittens and puppies) are born, their eyes are closed. They are helpless and need to stay close to their mother. They mostly eat and sleep. After a while, when their eyes are open and they are bigger, they are ready to be gently played with and can be outside on the grass. Eventually, the bunnies are large enough to eat rabbit food and can leave their mother. This is when it is time to find new homes for them.

Parent's Note

The Little Rabbit with the scenario of finding homes for a pet's babies is a prelude to a lesson in *Five in a Row*, Volume 3, *Andy and the Circus*. If you should happen to use that lesson later, you'll be able to say, "Remember when Sarah had to find homes for Sunday, Monday, Tuesday? etc.

Problem Solving

Sarah has to find homes for Buttercup's babies. This is her problem to solve. How does Sarah go about finding homes for her pet bunnies? (She speaks with her friends and finds homes through them.) Ask your older child if he can think of other ways Sarah might have found homes for the young bunnies. (This is an exercise in thinking of several different ways to solve a problem.) She could have posted a sign in a store or taken the box of bunnies to a place frequented by lots of people. Sarah could have then asked people if they would like to have a bunny for a pet. She could have run an advertisement in the paper or she could have made up fliers to put in people's doors in her neighborhood. Have your child watch for people advertising personal items and notice the different methods they use. Can your child think of any other ways Sarah might have solved her problem?

Language: Words

Look at the full-picture page where young Buttercup finds shelter from the rain under a rhubarb plant. She has found a natural umbrella!

Umbrella is a funny word. Consider the word umbrella and marvel at our rich language. One little girl, confused by the term, coined a new word—"rainbrella." That new word seemed to make more sense to her and it became her family's favorite preference. Making up or coining new words is a special thing within a family. If someone in your family coins special words, continue to use them and your family will have a few words of a special *secret* language that only you understand together!

Art

After reading the story, go back and look at each picture of Buttercup and her bunnies. Concentrate on all the different views that you have of the rabbits. There are front views, side views, and views from behind. If your child has a stuffed bunny, let him set the toy in different poses where he can view it from different directions like the pictures in the story.

Parent's Note

Judy and Phoebee Dunn have created other great titles for Random House. From time to time you might find another one to enjoy together with your child. *The Little Duck*, 1976 Random House, ISBN 0394832477, *The Little Lamb*, 1977 Random House, ISBN 0394834550 and *The Little Goat*, 1978 Random House, ISBN 0394838726. These stories all show families with pets and have bright photography and funny surprises! They have been well-loved stories for over twenty years.

Companion Story

The Little Rabbit is a story about a domestic pet bunny and the babies she raises. Jim Arnosky has written and illustrated a story about a wild rabbit raising her babies in the woods. Arnosky's book is called *Rabbits and Raindrops*, G. P. Putnam's Sons, New York, ISBN 0399226354. The illustrations are delightful and the stories somewhat parallel. Your child will delight in a look at rabbits from a "woodsy" view. This is a book too good to miss!

ASK MR. BEAR

Title: *Ask Mr. Bear*
Author: Marjorie Flack
Illustrator: Marjorie Flack
Copyright: 1932

Summary

This story, first published in 1932 has been enjoyed by generations of children. It is a boy's search for a gift for his mother and the special gift that he finds!

Bible

The little boy in *Ask Mr. Bear* wants to find the right gift. When he is sure he knows what it is, he gives it lovingly and cheerfully! 2 Corinthians 9:7 says that God loves a cheerful giver.

Problem Solving and Special Places

After reading the story together, look at the first picture with text. It shows Danny sitting on a step to think. After Danny thinks, what does he do next? (He decides to ask the advice of others, which is sometimes a good way to solve a problem. He does not *have* to act on their advice. His helpers only give suggestions. So, Danny continues until he finds just the right solution to his quest.)

Does your child have a favorite place that he can go to think—a thinking place? For some, it might be a favorite chair or on a step. For others it might be on a fence rail outdoors or a large rock. Some thinking places are more secret like a tree house, or under a table, etc. If you had a special place where *you* went to think things out, share it with your child.

Birthdays

By the age of three, birthdays begin to take on a special significance to a child. This is true of his own birthday and the birthdays of others. After an initial reading of the story you could discuss the topic of birthdays. How does your child feel about his own? How does he feel about the birthdays of others? Even at young ages, thinking about giving presents to people, deciding what to give, wrapping, etc., can be exciting and enjoyable. It provides an introduction to caring for others and for decision making. It takes time to think of a gift, earn the money and then go shopping. It can take even longer to make a special gift. Each idea that the animals suggest to Danny would have made a lovely gift, but his mother already had them. So, Danny works hard and continues to search until he finds just the right present.

Music

Have you ever heard of an "unbirthday?" The Disney version of *Alice in Wonderland* introduces the idea of an "unbirthday party." Assuming that no one in your family has an actual birthday that day, after you've read the story you could sing a rousing chorus of "Happy *Un*-Birthday To You!" or from the Disney version of *Alice* "A Very Merry Un-Birthday To You, To You!" Sing to each other with gusto. Then enjoy a frosted cupcake with a candle that your child can blow out and give each other a Big *Un*-Birthday Bear Hug! (Make it even more fun after reading the story, by having a frosted *muffin* and doing this activity for *breakfast*. What a way to start the day!)

Drama: Actions and Voices

There are a great many actions included in *Ask Mr. Bear* and you might wait with this activity to see if your child begins to act out some of these on his own. But, someday after reading the story you could suggest that he do the actions *along with* the accompanying animal voices. See if your child can walk quietly, then skip* while he clucks like a hen, hop while he clucks like a hen *and* honks like a goose, gallop* as he clucks like a hen, honks like a goose *and* maa's like a goat, etc., Include trotting while baa-ing, and running while moo-ing. Your young child may just want to do *one* of these actions.

*Skipping and galloping are more difficult skills that sometimes take a while to accomplish. Be encouraging, but not critical. Large motor skill accomplishments come at different times for different children. The key to this activity is fun. Maybe *you* could try these actions and animal sounds while your child watches. Be prepared for giggles.

Drama: Puppet Show

After enjoying a reading of the story together, you could bring out some prepared puppets for a show. These puppets could be finger puppets made from construction paper or decorated white paper. Or they could be more substantial cloth or papier mache in the shape of the animals, Danny and his mother. You could also design scenery for a backdrop using Danny's home for the beginning and end of the story. Another scene could have a simple backdrop of sky and grass where Danny talks to the animals. One final backdrop might show the woods where Danny will meet the bear and get his birthday idea! You can do this backdrop scenery on a large piece of paper or on poster board. You can do drawings or paintings that are quite simple, just to give the effect of these places. Or, you can make the scenery as sophisticated as you like. An easy way to create your own puppet theatre is to simply skirt a table with an old sheet or fabric. Then kneel down behind the table and use the tabletop for a puppet stage. Affix your backdrop to the wall behind your stage with teacher's tacky putty, loops of masking tape, push-pins, etc.

Use the puppets and scenery to act out a puppet show of this story. You can also have your child help you, or he can put on the show himself if he desires. If you think it is fun, have your child's friends or relatives over to watch. This kind of activity lays a foundation for your child's understanding of theatre and can be a creative drama experience in itself. Maybe you or your child would like to add more animals and birthday suggestions to the story. You might even want to come up with a different birthday present for the Mother.

Memory

After reading the story together, ask your child if he can remember all the gift suggestions that Danny received. (The suggestions were: an egg, a pillow, cheese, a blanket, milk and cream, and a hug.) If your child can't remember some of these, it might help if he can recall the animals that

talked to Danny. But, if he is very young and he remembers even *one* of the birthday suggestions, compliment him! On successive readings you may find that he can remember more.

Language: Rhyme

After enjoying the story, use the "gift idea" words and try to find rhymes for them. For instance: egg—beg, Meg, leg; pillow—willow, billow; cheese—please, peas, sneeze, trees; blanket—crank it, spank it; milk—silk, bilk; cream—scream, beam; hug—bug, mug, etc. Rhymes are fun anytime, but tying them to the words of a story can make the game even more interesting.

Science: Woodland Habitat

After reading the story, turn to the page where Danny meets the bear. Look at the woodland scene and talk about it. What do you see? What is in the woods? (ferns, toad or frog, mushrooms or toadstools, shadows—it's darker in the woods, lots of trees) Can you visit a woods near you? Maybe you might find squirrels, birds, etc. If you live far from any wooded area, find good books at the library (perhaps with photographs) that show the woodland life.

Art: Color

Enjoy the story with your child and then talk about the illustrations. The cover of the book is a bright yellow, but the pictures inside are what we call pastel shades. You don't necessarily need to teach this. Again you might get a giant box of crayons and let your child hunt for the pale pastel colors he sees in these illustrations. If you have a copy of the book *Goodnight Moon* by Margaret Wise Brown, compare the illustrations in the two books. Just comment to your child that one has *bright* colors like in his crayon box of eight fat crayons, while *Ask Mr. Bear* has the *pastels* he found in the larger box of colors.

Language: Poetry

Almost any story lends itself to interpretation in a poem or song. The story *Ask Mr. Bear* could inspire a rhyme like:

> *Birthday's here*
> *We need to find*
> *A gift for a friend* (or sister, brother, etc.)
> *Who's sweet and kind!*
>
> *What shall we find?*
> *We hope it's right,*
> *To fill our friend* (or sister, brother, etc.)
> *With pure delight!*

Hum along to this rhyme and a melody will probably appear. Voila! A song! These types of personally created tie-in's to a story are loved by children everywhere. Sing the song with your child whenever you shop for or make a birthday present.

Language: Sayings

Explore the phrase "bear hug" and remind your child it means "a long, tight squeeze" that is different from a light, quick hug. Give each other a bear hug!

BLUEBERRIES FOR SAL

Title: *Blueberries for Sal*
Author: Robert McCloskey
Illustrator: Robert McCloskey
Copyright: 1948
Award: Caldecott Honor Book

Summary

Sal is separated from her mother in a mighty "mix up" while on an outing to gather blueberries for the winter.

Bible: Health and Safety

Bible Verse: Where you go I will go (Ruth 1). In the story of Ruth, a young woman follows after her mother-in-law. Briefly retell this story to your child. Keep it very simple. Then remind him of the "careful following" that Ruth did as she followed after Naomi. In *Blueberries for Sal*, little Sal begins her day's berry picking following after her mother, keeping her in sight. But, as Sal becomes focused on the interesting things around her, she loses track of her mother. Talk with your child about the danger of becoming separated at a store, mall, etc. Discuss the necessity of being aware, keeping up with, and following his parents. Discuss what to do if separated, and make a plan. For a very young child, the echoing of Ruth's proclamation: "Where you go, I will go," might remind and help him to stay focused on following you.

Math

A small, tin pail would make this time spent together lots of fun! Sal picks, eats, and drops berries in her pail. Using blueberries (fun to eat) or other counting objects such as blocks, act out the scene on pages 8 and 9 of *Blueberries for Sal*. Introduce concepts of counting and present the idea of subtraction (taking away). "If you pick three berries and eat two of them, how many

berries do you have left?" etc. Keep it light and exclaim about how much fun math can be. A positive experience now will build a platform for future enjoyment of this subject.

If you use real blueberries, be sure to listen to the sound the berries make as they hit the bottom of the pail. *"Kuplink, kuplank, kuplunk!"*

History

This story was written many years ago. Look at the double-page picture of little Sal's kitchen inside the cover or before the title page. Does your child notice anything different from his own kitchen? The wood-burning stove is probably different. Just for fun, take the book to the kitchen and point out some of the differences. (Your kitchen probably has either natural gas or electric power and no flue or wood box.)

If you don't care to draw a very young child's attention to potentially dangerous stoves and ovens, try discussing the open drawer in the picture of Sal's kitchen. In it is an old-fashioned egg beater. Explain how it worked and show your child your electric mixer or wire wisks, etc.

Another clue to the age of the story is Sal's family car pictured on page 6. Has your child seen automobiles that look like this? Do most of the cars today look like this? Your child may not be overly responsive during this type of discussion, but later he may be more inclined to notice the types

of vehicles around him because you have drawn his attention to the fact that not all cars are alike.

Classification

Being able to classify items is an important life skill. We understand much of the world around us as we learn to classify and group similar items and ideas together. Young children can learn early classifying skills and have fun at the same time. In the above lesson we talked about cars and the fact that all cars are not alike. As your child is noticing the differences, he might notice that cars can be put in different groups. One way to group cars is by color, i.e., all the red ones, blue ones, green ones, etc. Or they could be separated by body style such as two-door, four-door, hatchbacks, station wagons, vans, convertibles, sedans, and sports cars. If you happen to have a collection of toy cars and trucks, your young child might have fun grouping them as you call out different categories. Categories could also include, vehicles used for doing work like a tow-truck; vehicles used primarily for pleasure, like a two-seat sports car, etc. (Or you can laminate and cut out pictures of cars, trucks, construction equipment, etc., from magazines. Your child can sort these *pictures* as well.) Another way to play this game is for your child to secretly choose a group category, arrange the cars and have you guess what his category is. Either way, this is a game that provides fun as well as subtle learning experiences.

Young children can also match socks and make piles according to which socks belong to which member of the family and other enjoyable tasks that begin the skill of classification.* See Science, Zoology.

Two Stories in One

In the story of *Blueberries for Sal,* there are two stories: one of the bear cub and its mother and one of little Sal and her mother. After a reading of the story, you might mention that there seem to be *two* stories. Talk over how the story would have been different if the bears had not been involved. The story might have been something like this: Little Sal and her mother went to pick blueberries to can for the winter. Little Sal wasn't paying attention and soon her mother was out of sight. She saw a crow and eventually found her mother again. Ask your child if he would have liked that story. If, instead, he likes the story the way Robert McCloskey wrote it, gently see if he can give any reasons why. (He may think the mix-up is humorous, or he may think that it is kind of scary and it makes the story more interesting. Or he may not know—he just likes it! and that is fine.)

Science: Botany

Talk about the blueberry bushes and the kind of trees you see in the illustrations (pine-type evergreens). Let your child point out some of these as you turn the pages. Are these kinds of trees and shrubs common in your area? Go outside for a little "nature walk" with your child and explore the types of trees in *your* neighborhood.

Science: Zoology

How many different animals can you find in the pictures? Can your child name some of them? (Animals include a partridge, crow and bear.) Talk about bears. You could already be prepared with a very simple book from the library about bears. Read it together or just look at the pictures. If there is intense interest in this subject, many libraries have available (or on request) videotapes about bears which will add an audio-visual dimension to your discussion. Make sure you preview the videos.

*Suggestions were made in above lessons to begin teaching simple, enjoyable classification skills. Animals and plants are classified into different groups and you might want to use index cards to begin an introductory classification game. Animals might be introduced in this way: Search each *Before Five in a Row* story that you read and as you encounter various animals draw or cut out pictures of the animals and place one on each card. Wildlife magazines are great for this kind of project, as well as reproducible art clip illustrations and computer software programs with copyright free art clips. After you have a small stack of cards, group the birds together, the mammals together, etc. You don't have to teach the grouping name. Maybe just discuss the similarities, such as, "Which of these cards show animals that have wings and a beak?" And then group those together. Or, "Which have fur, four legs, etc." From an early age, your child can have fun realizing that fish don't go in the "birds" card pile and that mammal-type animals are different from snakes. As you read more and more of the stories,

the game becomes longer as the stack of cards grows. Remember that this is meant to be a very brief, colorful, enjoyable *introduction* to the world of classification, presented as a game rather than educational instruction.

Art

Talk about the blue ink illustrations and spend some time looking at them together. Does your child wish the pictures were in color or does he enjoy these pictures just as much? What is your child's favorite picture? Show him yours.

For an art project, have your child draw a mountain. Then if he desires, he can draw little Sal on one side and little bear on the other. If he is not ready for such detail, paste cut outs of Little Sal and the bear on his drawn mountain. Let him add any details he wishes. Maybe some blueberry bushes would be nice.

Music

When Sal first began to pick the blueberries they hit the bottom of the empty tin pail with a *"Kuplink, kuplank, kuplunk!"* sound. This sound has rhythm possibilities. Together, clap your hands to the sound of the words. Try different rhythms and tempos. Hum the words for a while and then try composing a little song to sing about the berries hitting the bottom of the pail and the sound they make! Enjoy this time of creativity and laugh a lot!

GOODNIGHT MOON

Title: *Goodnight Moon*
Author: Margaret Wise Brown
Illustrator: Clement Hurd
Copyright: 1947

Summary

Gentleness and rhythmic calm prevail as a young bunny prepares for bedtime and says goodnight to each familiar object in his room, including the moon in his window!

Bible

Read Psalm 127:2b about God giving to His beloved, even in their sleep. It is a wonder to consider that even while sleeping, the Lord is aware and giving. Discuss this idea with your child.

Or you can read Genesis 1:14-19 and share with your child briefly about the creation of the sun, moon and stars which took place on the fourth day of creation.

Art

Notice with your child the first picture of the story. The room is lighted (from the fireplace and at least one lamp) so the outside, beyond the window looks very *dark*. In the last picture, the room is dark and now the outside looks *bright*. Looking through the pictures in-between, does it slowly become lighter outside? No, it just *appears* lighter as the room becomes darker. At night you can show your child how this concept works, as our eyes become accustomed to the dark and the outside lights seem brighter.

Bright primary and secondary colors are used in this art work. You may want to take this opportunity to learn red, yellow and blue as the primary colors. If there is a great deal of interest, and if your child is inquiring about the green used, you can decide if going on to teach the secondary colors and how they are derived from the primary colors is appropriate at this time.

On the third double-page, color illustration, there is a picture hanging on the wall over the doll-house and bookcase. It looks like a bunny fishing for a bunny. The picture is from another book written by the author of *Goodnight Moon,* called *The Runaway Bunny.* The same illustrator, Clement Hurd, created the pictures for both books. If your child knows *Runaway Bunny,* he will recognize the picture of the bunny fisherman. If not, *Runaway Bunny* is included in the lesson plans of this manual and when you get to that book, reread *Goodnight Moon* and see if your child notices the picture!

Science: Zoology

Talk about and point out different kinds of animals included in the text or illustrations of *Goodnight Moon.* Look in the text for new animals to add to your classification game begun in *Blueberries for Sal.* You may want to make additional index cards for cows, bears, mice, elephants, giraffes, cats, rabbits, etc.

Memory

Play a memory game. First, read the story. Then look at the picture of the room. Close the book and try to remember as many items and details as possible.

Literature: Nursery Rhymes

The story makes reference to the nursery rhyme "Hey Diddle Diddle" where the "cow jumps over the moon." If your child isn't familiar with this rhyme, it might be a good time to share it with him. Nursery rhymes can provide beginning "sound" recognition and introduce the appreciation of rhyming poetry. Also, just as there was an allusion to a well known rhyme in this story, there are many references made in literature to famous nursery rhymes. So, the knowledge of them increases your child's cultural literacy. In other words, as your child is presented with these references, he will recognize the source and often appreciate the reason why an author included such rhymes in his story.

Literature: Storytelling

In the first illustration, there is a picture on the wall of three bears sitting in chairs. Does your child know the story of *Goldilocks and the Three Bears*? If not, you might want to share it now. Your child will then recognize the source of the three bears picture in future readings of *Goodnight Moon.*

Another storytelling project you might want to try is to use the *pattern* of story line in *Goodnight Moon*. In this way, your child might make up a story about saying "Hello" to everything around him in the morning. The light would get brighter and brighter and each item could be mentioned as the room "awakened."

Parent's Note

Like Margaret Wise Brown, Eloise Wilkin has written another wonderful "goodnight" book that you might like to find. It is called *My Goodnight Book*, 1981 Golden Press, ISBN 0307122581. It comes in the hard cardboard, young child's format and has beautiful, soothing pictures.

Vocabulary

This story uses the word *great* to mean big. Talk with your older child about this usage and also other ways to use great, such as great meaning fantastic, or great meaning influential or powerful, etc.

Shapes

Goodnight Moon has many shapes represented in the illustrations. Talk about circles, squares, triangles, etc., and let your child look for these shapes as he examines the illustrations during future readings.

Art

If your child loves this story and would enjoy having a *Goodnight Moon* print, you can order one from your local bookstore. Ask for ISBN 1568900856 from Harper and Row.

THE BIG GREEN POCKETBOOK

Title: *The Big Green Pocketbook*
Author: Candice Ransom
Illustrator: Felicia Bond
Copyright: 1993

Summary

An outing with Mama provides a young girl the chance to "collect her morning" in a big green pocketbook.

Bible

One of the experiences in this story, is the tragic loss of the little girl's pocketbook, her desire to find it because it so important to her, and the rejoicing once it is found. After all, it had her entire "morning" in it. This reminds us of the story of the woman and the lost coin. Found in Luke, chapter 15, the verses tell the story of a lady who loses a coin, searches diligently for it and rejoices when it is found. The "Woman and the Lost Coin" is a parable and also can be used to share other truths of the Kingdom.

Another avenue for discussing Bible truths is the kindness of the people in the story who give the young girl items for her pocketbook and the bus driver who does the good deed of the day, taking the time and effort to return the beloved pocketbook. You might want to examine Galations 5:22-23 about the fruit of the Spirit (kindness, etc.). You can also read about the many acts of kindness, such as the story of Dorcas (Acts 9:36), the parable of the Good Samaritan (Luke 10), etc.

Literature: Storytelling

Boys or girls can imagine the same story line with a backpack instead of a pocketbook. They can imagine what would be in the backpack if they collected things on all *their* outings.

Art

After reading the story, you could talk about the colors Felicia Bond used, especially the bright green that is predominant in the illustrations. Ask your child if he thinks this color green is cheerful. Your child could experiment with yellow and blue paint, making the bright green for fun, or use a bright chartreuse marker or colored pencil and just make designs.

Look at the trees on the title page. Ask your child why they seem to be bent over. These illustrations show the effect of the wind. When you are on outings, point out trees that are bent in the breeze.

Last of all, look at the picture where the girl is sitting on the floor with her back to the reader. Talk about how she might be feeling. Perhaps she is feeling disappointment, grief or anger. Perhaps she is calmly praying that her pocketbook will be found. Any of these ideas could be correct, and it might be helpful for your child to think about the different ways we can react to a crisis.

Stores

How many stores and businesses appeared in this story? See if your child can remember some of the places that the mother and daughter visited (drugstore, dry cleaners, dime store, bank, jewelry store, insurance office, etc.). Talk about what goes on in one or two of these places. If your child has never been in a jewelry store or dry cleaners,

take him for a visit. Most of the time we take our children along with us while we try to accomplish the items on our agenda. Planning a special trip to a store or mall now and then that is simply for our child may be a new idea. If you decide to visit a jewelry store just to show your child what that type of store is like, you will probably be far more focused on him. You will point things out to each other and have time to listen to his comments and questions without the worry of all the things you need to get done. These are trips that make memories and help a child feel special.

Also, you may want to ride a bus together just for the fun of it. The little girl describes her bus with a hot cloud coming out of it as the door opens, leather seats creaking, and a cloud of brown dust as it drives away. If you take a bus ride, ask your child to think of some of the sights, smells, sounds, etc., connected with *his* bus ride.

Manners

The Big Green Pocketbook provides a wonderful forum to discuss manners, from how one is to act in public, to being grateful and remembering to say thank you. The young girl even takes the time to draw a special thank you picture for the bus driver. Is there someone your child can thank for an act of kindness?

Details

In the illustrations on the page where Mama visits the jewelry store, there is a man with a dog named Max. (How do we *know* the dog's name is Max? Look carefully at the illustration!) Ask your child where the man has been. Based on his armload of food, your child might guess he's been to the grocery store. What kind of shoes is the man wearing? On the page where Mama stops at the bank, what are the names of the bank tellers? The next time you visit the bank with your child you can point out the teller's name-plates, just like in the story of the big green pocketbook!

Zoology

If you're playing the animal classification game begun in the lessons for *Blueberries for Sal*, add koala and a dog to your cards.

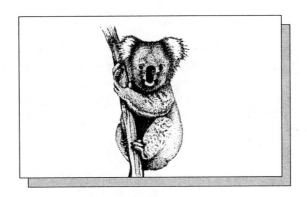

Shapes

Felicia Bond illustrated this story using many different shapes. The young girl's shirt on the front cover has rectangles, semicircles and triangles. There is a stop sign in the background with an octagon shape. Cooking pans on the drugstore wall appear as ovals. If you have discussed different shapes with your child, have him look through the pictures for objects that show a variety of shapes.

THE RUNAWAY BUNNY

Title: *The Runaway Bunny*
Author: Margaret Wise Brown
Illustrator: Clement Hurd
Copyright: 1942

Summary

How far will love reach? The nonchalant baby bunny finds the comforting truth as he and his mother imagine different situations.

Bible

The Runaway Bunny illustrates the meaning of Jeremiah 31:3 where the Bible declares that God's love is everlasting and that He draws us with lovingkindness. In Psalm 139, God assures us that no matter *where* we go He will follow us, just like the mother bunny in our story.

Science: Zoology

Look for new animals and add pictures to your classification index cards. (You'll find a fish and a monkey. Can you find others?) These cards can be used in the animal classification game begun in the lesson plans for *Blueberries for Sal*.

Science: Botany

What happened to the tree in the first color illustration of the story? (It died and fell down. Perhaps it was diseased or maybe it was struck by lightning. Many fallen decayed trees become homes for various birds and other animals, along with a multitude of insects.) Perhaps you have an old dead tree that you could examine. Look for animals and insects living there. Sometimes when trees die, people replace them with new, young trees. Consider planting a tree with your child. Let him finish patting the dirt around the tree and helping to water it. As it grows, he will remember this special time spent together.

Learning a new word

Did your child notice the *scarecrow* shown in the color picture after the last page of text? Explain to him that scarecrows are created by farmers in order to keep birds from eating the seeds in the garden. If you have Beatrix Potter's own illustrations in *The Tale of Peter Rabbit* you'll find another picture of a scarecrow!

Art

In The Runaway Bunny Clement Hurd has used both pen and ink sketches and color paintings to show the imaginings of the author's story. Ask your child which pictures he likes best. Perhaps he senses a beauty about both kinds. If you like, you might use this opportunity to teach or review colors, especially pink and purple, or to find many different shades of green. A giant box of crayons or a large chart from a oil-paint or watercolor company can be useful in this kind of color exploration. Your child can find many shades of color to correspond to the illustrations in the story.

Find the double-page, color illustration where the mother rabbit has her son on her lap in a rocking chair. Did your child notice the picture on the wall? It's the same picture of the cow jumping over the moon that was on the wall in *Goodnight Moon*! Remember that *Goodnight Moon* had a picture of the mother rabbit fishing for her son in the trout stream from *Runaway Bunny*! Your child might not react to this picture exchange, or he might find it extremely interesting and amus-

ing. Remind him that it is the same artist/illustrator that created the pictures for both books.

Math: Shapes

You can add crescent to the shapes you've discussed. Also, you could use this story to explain the difference between a disk (like a pizza or a compact disc), a circle (a circular line drawn on paper), and a sphere (like a ball), even though we call all these shapes round! Let your child draw a circle or take a piece of yarn tied together into a loop and make a circle on the table with it. Then let him handle a plate, or CD, etc., and finally, a ball. Checkers would be an example of a disk, while the round knob on the top of your staircase post is a sphere. Look for examples from time to time of the many shapes around you.

In the story of *The Runaway Bunny* there are some examples of spheres. In the flower garden picture, the top of the stone wall has a stone ball, or sphere. In the rocking chair picture there is a ball of yarn on the floor and the last color illustration has the full moon over the field. This doesn't look much like a sphere, but after having explored the moon, we know that it too is spherical. It may interest some children to know that the moon, even though it appears flat like a disk is actually a sphere! It is enough for a very young child to know that *round* is a word used when considering objects such as a CD or a checker, as well as when discussing circles or balls (spheres).

Memory Game

After reading the story together, ask your child how many different things the young bunny imagines he could be? (He imagines he could be a fish, a rock on a mountain, crocus in a hidden garden, a bird, a sailboat, a trapeze artist, and a boy.) What does his mother imagine she could be? (She imagines she could be a fisherman, a mountain climber, a gardener, a tree, the wind, a tightrope walker, and a mother.)

THE ABC BUNNY

Title: *The ABC Bunny*
Author: Wanda Gag
Illustrator: Wanda Gag
Copyright: 1933

Summary

An inquisitive bunny and a mad dash through the alphabet is set in lyrical rhyme that has delighted children for over sixty years!

Bible

Because the alphabet is a concept that has an order, such as "a" comes before "b," etc., you might want to use a concordance to find verses about "order" or "orderliness." Look at the verse about doing things right and in order, 1 Corinthians 14:40. Or you could talk about the "order" in creation. What did God do first? Second? etc.

Science: Botany

From *The ABC Bunny*, you may explore such plant life as: apples, flowers, seeds, leaves, a tree stump and "greens!"

Science: Weather

After reading the story, you may want discuss weather phenomena such as lightning, clouds, wind, hail, and sun. Begin observing and discussing the weather with your child on a regular basis.

Science: Zoology

Add to your classification game with new index cards for: blue jay, lizard, insect, squirrel, frog, owl, porcupine, and quail. (The classification game was begun and explained in the lesson plans for *Blueberries for Sal*.)

Art

Wanda Gag (her name rhymes with Bog, not Bag), probably used charcoal or pencil for her illustrations. The lines and tones are soft and inviting. Look at the swirls of lines on every page. The background, made up of these lines, always seems to be in motion. For a young child who shows an interest in art, you might examine Van Gogh's *Starry Night* together and talk about the similarities.

Notice, too, the body action of the bunny, including his expressions. There is an abundance of action here! Have your child try a bit of drama by pretending he's a bunny, and act out as many of *The ABC Bunny's* actions as he can.

Printing Colors

The cover is printed in what three colors? (Black, red and green.) Questions like this are more than just asking your child to name the three colors. In addition, these types of questions help him focus his attention. He may never have noticed that the cover was a three color printing. (Remember, the white of the paper doesn't count.) Becoming increasingly aware of details is a significant learning skill. To continue helping him "see" what is on the pages before him, call attention to the song page which is red and black ink, and the illustrations for the story which are black ink only, with each letter printed in red.

Math: Counting

There are many objects your older child might enjoy counting such as bunnies, hail stones, flowers, etc. From time to time, after reading the story, select one or two objects and go through the book carefully, page by page, as your child counts. If your child is too young to count independently, now and then, when you read count for him and let him follow along. (*One is One* by Tasha Tudor is a brightly illustrated counting book that you would enjoy reading with your child.)

Language: The Alphabet

Of course just reading this book to your young child will allow him to *hear* over and over the names of the letters of the alphabet. There are many other delightful alphabet books which you can read to your child long before you attempt to "teach" him the alphabet. He will enjoy these alphabet books, and find the *sounds* of the letters familiar when he is older and ready to learn to read.

When you are ready to teach *sight* recognition for each letter, borrow the idea from the back cover of *The ABC Bunny*. Take a large sheet of paper and make leaves containing letters of the alphabet for your older child to point to and recite. For beginning recognition you might have a page full of leaves and fill them all in with the same specific letter until he knows and recognizes that letter. Now add a second letter, etc. A more advanced plan would be to make the letters in a random pattern, like the book cover, in either upper or lower case, and work on letter recognition.

Letter recognition is one thing, but when does your child learn to read and write? Let's examine the process of learning. Many times learning results from frustrations. For instance a baby is content for a time to view the world while lying on his back or on his stomach. But, as his muscles strengthen and he becomes bored and frustrated, he learns to turn himself over. Voila! A new view! The motivation for wanting to turn over is dissatisfaction or frustration.

In the same way, a young child enjoys crawling for a time. Then his muscles strengthen, his coordination improves and he notices others moving quickly on two feet. He now becomes frustrated with crawling and begins to explore walking.

There is a similar process with reading and writing. Between the ages of two and four your child will probably be content with his "own" writing-- his *marvelous* scribbles. Remember how convinced *you* were that you were actually writing? Let your child have this enjoyable time. There is no need to push academics. When he makes his own discovery (usually around four or five) that his writing isn't communicative to the adult world, he will become frustrated. This desire is what naturally propels him to learn his letters and begin to write. *He* feels the need—he is *motivated* to do the work—he learns *happily*! Read

Bunny Cakes by Rosemary Wells to witness these concepts in action! In this story, Max can still communicate with pictures so he is not *quite* frustrated enough to be ready for writing lessons, but he is *so* close!

Remember when leading your child toward academic pursuits that there is not a prize for getting there first! The important thing is your child's character and your relationship with him, all the other academic achievements will follow in time.

Sounds: Rhymes

While reading the story together with your child, enjoy the sounds of words like Crash! Dash! and Flash! Look for other rhyming words and make up some of your own.

Music

Try the song at the beginning of the story. The music was written by Wanda Gag's sister. Sing the song, clap the rhythm, stamp the rhythm and then change the tempo and try it again.

Talk about the funny shapes that do not look like letters. These are musical notes. Continue to point out musical notes when you see them in hymnals, magazines, on wrapping paper or wherever they might appear.

IF JESUS CAME TO MY HOUSE

Title: *If Jesus Came to My House*
Author: Joan Gale Thomas
Illustrated: Joan Gale Thomas
Copyright: 1951

Summary

An imaginary visit from a most special visitor brings out the best in the host and teaches him how to care for the people around him.

Bible

This warm and gracious story in verse brings with it a chance to explore the Golden Rule (Matthew 7:12.) You can also discuss the idea of "doing it to the least of these" as found in Matthew 25:40. Another verse that would fit in with this story is Hebrews 13:2a with its reminder to not neglect showing hospitality to strangers!

Science: Shadows

The incident in the story where the child is frightened by the shadows in the hall gives you a chance to discuss shadows. By calling your very young child's attention to shadows, you are laying the groundwork and helping to develop an interest in science lessons in later years. You do not need to try to explain what makes shadows. Instead, just have fun making some. You could even try this in a hallway! Or, on a sunny day, stand out in the yard in the early morning and demonstrate how distorted (taller than life) the shadows are. Try this exercise again near noon time and see how the shadow has become shorter. Because the angle of light distorts true sizes, over-sized shadows can sometimes be quite frightening. Then, too, the indefinite character of shadow lines are often scary. Demonstrate how to make hand shadows of different animals. Look for shadows in other picture books, and paintings, etc.

Imagining and Poetry

Find the picture where the boy points out his favorite places in the house. He says there is a hole behind the stairs where he pretends he is a mouse. Does your child have any special places where he can pretend? Besides favorite places in the house, large cardboard boxes can also be easily converted into clubhouses, cars, buses, caves, ships, etc., for additional special places of imagining.

The boy in the story mentions shadows. Robert Louis Stevenson wrote a poem about shadows, called *I Have a Little Shadow*. It begins, "I have a little shadow that goes in and out with me...." Look for it in children's poetry anthologies or in the works of Robert Louis Stevenson. It is included in the Dover Coloring Book: *A Child's Garden of Verses Coloring Book*, ISBN 0486234819. This poem has a pleasing rhythm and rhyme, and deals with the subject of shadows in a delightful way. It has been a childhood favorite for several generations.

Hospitality

Obviously *If Jesus Came to My House* is a book about learning to be sociable through learning hospitality. It addresses how to greet someone at the door, invite him in, share with him the best of everything, serve him refreshment, accompany him to the door or gate, invite him to come back again and how to say good-bye. Reading a book like this one by Joan Gale Thomas begins to teach young children these social graces. But even more importantly, they will quickly copy proper social behavior which you model for them. Have fun with this book. Enjoy the rhyme and the gentle spirit of this story poem. You may have fun acting out some of the verses in the story.

Art

The illustrations are pen and ink with red accents. Have fun pointing out the red on each page. As you read the story, look for the dog. He only appears in certain illustrations. In illustrations three and four, the crackling fireplace gives a cozy feeling. Think about the things that make you feel warm and cozy, perhaps a cup of tea or cocoa, or a soft blanket, etc. Ask your child what gives him cozy feelings. Snuggle together as you read the story again.

Fears

After reading the story, talk about the little boy who says that sometimes he is afraid in the dark area of the hall where the shadows are. Everyone is afraid of something at some time. Just letting a child know that fear is a feeling that *everyone* experiences takes away some of its sting. But we have also been given help. In the Bible we are instructed to "fear not." and to remember that God is with us, Isaiah 41:10. Indeed, the little boy in the story says later that he doesn't have to be afraid because he knows that Jesus is near. It takes time to understand, believe and apply this truth. A child who has patient, loving parents who take time to let him grow in this truth is indeed blessed.

Music

Music is a precious gift. There are many occasions when men look to music to supply emotional benefit. Remember the song "Whistle While You Work"? The music is supposed to help the work go faster and in a more enjoyable manner. Music is used when we are happy and feel celebratory, when we are sad and when we are afraid. Music can soothe as a lullaby or motivate like a march.

(In this story the little boy is afraid of the shadows.) Singing a song can help relieve fears. Encourage your child by singing with him often, in happy times as well as fearful ones.

CAPS FOR SALE

Title: *Caps for Sale*
Author: Esphyr Slobodkina
Illustrated: Esphyr Slobodkina
Copyright: 1940

Summary:

There are many different ways to solve problems. Sometimes the solution is merely an accident!

Bible

Proverbs 6:10 and 11 suggest that sleeping on the job might cause problems!

Math: Counting

Ask your child how many there are of each colored hat. How many monkeys? You could introduce a brief introductory lesson on money. The caps in this story sold for fifty cents. Your older child might be amazed at the fact that he could pay for one of these hats with fifty pennies, ten nickles, five dimes, two quarters or one half-dollar. It is not necessary for your child to try to memorize this information, but just be introduced to it for his own enjoyment.

Language: Vocabulary

A *bunch* of something is many or several. A *cap* is another name for hat. These simple words may be new to your young child.

Sayings

You may want to explain the saying: "Monkey see, monkey do." Monkeys often mimic the actions they see in humans. (Note—the phrase "Monkey see, monkey do," never actually is said in the story. Rather, it is acted out.) Are there other sayings you could discuss, such as "early to bed...", or maybe a unique, private, family saying? Special secret family sayings build intimacy and bring a sense of humor and enjoyment to life.

Science: Health

The man walking along balancing his hats is reminiscent of the old-fashioned posture lessons where a child walked around with a book on his head. Your child might like to try balancing one or more items on his head while standing straight and tall. Let him try walking and see if he can keep his good posture.

Art

During another reading, look with your child at the first illustration (not the title page). See the man with the hats on his head? He is facing the reader, and there are houses, an orchard, and a church. Now turn to the last illustration. The man is facing away from the reader in the same scene and the gate has swung shut with the words: THE END written on it. Your child may appreciate the opening/closing aspect of these illustrations and someday he may write and illustrate a story with pictures that show a beginning and an ending. For now it is enough to mention the symbolism and enjoy it together.

The man with the hats has an unusual mustache. Share with your child that this type of mustache is called a *handlebar* mustache because it is long and curving, like the handlebars of an old-fashioned bicycle. You may be surprised as your child

finds other examples of people with handlebar mustaches in books, magazines, billboards, or movies, and points them out to you. With every new discovery, his knowledge and understanding of his world are increasing.

Another time, ask your child if the man always stacked the hats on his head in the same order? (He did. His checkered cap came first, then the bunch of gray ones, then a bunch of brown ones, followed by a bunch of blue ones, and last, the red caps on top.) What is missing from the stack on the cover? The bunch of brown ones and the checkered cap in his hand.

What is different about the tree under which the man slept from all the other trees in the background? The tree has very few leaves and no fruit. Perhaps the illustrator felt that the monkeys and hats needed to be more prominent.

Character

When the man awakens to find his hats missing, how do you think he feels? (Perhaps he feels baffled, afraid, etc.) After he tries to get the monkeys to give the hats back, how does he seem to feel? (Perhaps he is now feeling frustrated, angry, furious, etc.) What does he finally do? (He throws his hat on the ground.) Discuss feelings and the appropriate ways to handle frustrations and anger which are felt by everyone at sometime. Discuss the fact that feeling angry in certain situations isn't wrong in itself. Denying the feelings or trying not to be angry isn't as productive as admitting the "feeling," and learning limits to keep it from being harmful. Parents and teachers can model acceptable limits themselves by admitting when they are angry and saying that they are taking a break, maybe in a separate room, to calm down and think of solutions to the problem that is upsetting them.

Parent's Note

If you have enjoyed *Caps for Sale*, please try *The Wonderful Feast*. This is another book by Esphyr Slobodkina. It was written in 1955 and still maintains a bright, cheerful spot in children's literature. Currently in publication by Greenwillow Press, ISBN 068812349X. You and your child will enjoy it!

THE CARROT SEED

Title: *The Carrot Seed*
Author: Ruth Krauss
Illustrator: Crockett Johnson
Copyright: 1945

Summary

Sometimes it is important to work carefully and *never* give up.

Bible

You might want to briefly discuss the Parable of the Sower in the book of Luke and especially the verse in Luke 8:15. Also, you might find how the verses about having faith like a grain of mustard seed (Matthew 17 or Luke 17) could apply. There are many verses about patience, but it seems that the general counsel of scripture is that good things will come to those who wait.

Character

The boy and his family showed different types of character in this story. Ask your child if he can think of any reason why the boy's parents and brother told him the carrot wouldn't come up? Maybe they didn't want the boy to be disappointed. But, disappointment is something everyone has to face at times. Ask your child what the boy could have done if the carrot hadn't come up? He could have cried and given up. Or he could have planted another seed and tried to figure out what else he needed to do to have it succeed. The rest of the family doesn't seem to have a vision for the project and without vision there isn't much hope. But, the boy believes in his work and he is rewarded for his labors and patience.

Art

Notice that the illustrator has used pale orange and brown for every picture in the story except one. Which one? In the last illustration the prize carrot is *bright* orange!

Notice too, that the pictures are drawn flat (two-dimensional, without roundness from shading) like pictures from a coloring book, and the people are viewed from the side (*profile*).

Have fun watching the pupil of the boy's eye going up and down as he looks at the older people in the story and then back down to his carrot seed. There is humor in the pictures where the sprouting carrot just begins to rumble in the ground and in the next page of the carrot top.

Science: Seeds

The phenomenon of a seed sprouting is one of the miracles of life. Gather as many different kinds of seeds as possible and look at the variety. Soak some bean seeds in water overnight and then watch them sprout in dirt along the side of a glass jar or in a wet paper towel. The book, *Linnea's Windowsill Garden* by Christina Bjork, has many ideas that you might use with your child. Beyond seeds, don't forget the wonder *you* felt when you saw carrot tops growing their greenery in a saucer of water on your mother's windowsill. Try this with *your* child, too. (Cut off the top 1/2" of a carrot and place it cut-side-down, half-submerged in a saucer of water. Now wait for the green tops to grow!)

Science

One day, after reading *The Carrot Seed*, discuss with your older child the fact that certain seeds, such as beans for instance, germinate in as little as five days. Tiny carrot seeds, on the other hand, take about 21 days to germinate. It is because of this longer germination period that carrots are more difficult to grow. A gardener must take extra care to keep the weeds, which grow rapidly, from overwhelming the young carrots. In addition to weeding, watering is also critical for a longer period of time.

Care Giving

The young boy in *The Carrot Seed* has to work hard for many days to raise his carrot. Maybe there were some days when the boy is tired or wishes he could do something else, yet, he never waivers from his task. Whether we are caring for people, pets or plants there are many times when we must provide that care whether we feel like it or not. To be a care-giver requires consistency, even when we don't feel like working. Again, these ideas can be discussed, and they are easily caught as they are modeled by the parent who might say aloud at times, "I might not want to do this just now, but I need to do a good job whether I feel like it or not." Now and then you can also encourage your child to "keep to a task" just like the "boy who grew the carrot!"

Science: Gardening

After reading the story one day, let your child work in a prepared area of earth, planting some seeds. In the preceding lesson we learned about a carrot seed's characteristics and gardening needs. Your child can spend much of his excess energy in the wonderful pursuit of gardening. See to it that he has strong gardening tools, trowel, shovel, etc., and a small area where he can actually use them. (For your very young child, a few square feet of dirt and a strong spoon to dig with is enough.) Your older child, however, will want to see gardening *results*. Help him with carrots if he insists, but also with easier-to-grow seeds like sunflower, zinnia (butterflies love zinnias!), squash, etc. Some of these can even be grown in a large pot, if there is no small parcel of earth available. Fresh air, working muscles, lots of patience, and the hope of results make gardening a wonderful activity for your child. Don't do the work for him, but encourage him, by providing necessary materials in any way you can. Praise him for his efforts! For some children, the love of gardening, begun at age three or four, will last for a lifetime!

Science: Growth

Your child is growing, too! To chart his growth, take a roll of wide white paper and draw on it a five foot tall carrot. Paint the carrot bright orange and the carrot top green. Mark off feet and inches with a black marker. Attach the growth chart inside the door of your child's room or on the inside of his closet door, etc. Now and then have him stand tall and record his height. He will be excited as he sees his *own* progress!

THE SNOWY DAY

Title: *The Snowy Day*
Author: Ezra Jack Keats
Illustrator: Ezra Jack Keats
Award: Caldecott Award Book
Copyright: 1962

Summary

A winsome look at a boy's play and thoughts about the snow.

Bible

In the story *The Snowy Day*, the boy discovers the unique wonder of each day. He looks, touches, plays, experiments, learns, and enjoys. There is a verse that says we are to number our days so that a heart of wisdom might be lifted up to the Lord, Psalm 90:12. Part of this verse deals with the concept of making the most of each day and not missing any of the wonders and activities, as well as living carefully in the ways of the Lord. It is, among other things, an encouragement to be in all ways, alert!

Art

The pictures are a combination of watercolor and collage. Ezra Jack Keats has mixed two distinctly different mediums for his pictures. Your child might enjoy making some pictures or designs using watercolors and bits of colored paper just like Keats. Colored tissue wrapping paper can be useful here. Buy a multi-color pack. Let your child tear small pieces from different colors and glue them on a piece of white paper or a white paper plate. He can overlap the colors if he wishes. Then, a few drops of water dripped over the top of the work can make some interesting effects. Try several different techniques.

Science

How many kinds of weather did your child hear about in this story? Snowy weather and sunny weather were both mentioned in the text. Can your child name other types of weather? How about rainy, foggy weather, hail and sleet?

Snowflakes have six main points. Look at the double-page of snowflakes before the title page. Count the six main points. Why does snow melt? The story said the sun melted it, but actually, sun or not, temperatures above 32° Fahrenheit will melt snow or ice.

The boy makes funny tracks when he walks in the snow and when he drags the stick along beside him. You can see tracks in areas with dust, mud, or snow. Look for bird, cat, dog tracks, etc. If you live in a rural area, or near a wooded area, look alongside creeks or riverbanks for the tracks of wild animals. Your child can make his *own* shoe print or barefoot print by walking across wet grass and onto dry pavement.

Health

Did your child like the bright red snow suit that the boy wore to keep warm? Talk about wearing appropriate clothing during the different seasons. What would happen if the boy wore the red snow suit in the hot summer? In the winter, heavier clothing keeps us warm and can help prevent illness. In the spring and fall, depending on where you live, you might need to be aware of quick temperature changes. And in the summer, if the temperature is warm, lighter clothing is worn to keep the body from overheating. Just for fun, turn to page 32, the last page of text, and look at the two figures walking in the snow. Which one is Peter? How do you know? The red snow suit is a giveaway here.

Talk about the stop-light signal, the bright colors, and what they mean. Point out such light signals when you are on outings. Discuss the signal information, which is essential in knowing when to cross a street.

Maturity

Peter realizes that he was not yet old enough to join in the big boys' snowball fight. Was Peter willing to wait till he was older? He seems to be willing to wait and finds other things to do such as building a snowman, making snow angels, and having fun pretending. He proves that we can either spend our time being upset or find alternatives. Which sounds like more fun?

Memories

When Peter is getting ready for his bath, he tells his mother about his day's adventures. And when he takes his bath, he thinks and thinks about the exciting things he has done. Half the fun of having wonderful adventures is remembering them afterward. Sometimes we can have adventures alone; sometimes with friends or family. Tell your child about some of the adventures from your childhood, adding as many sights, sounds, smells, etc., as you can remember. Maybe he will tell you a few of his.

Remember *The Big Green Pocketbook* (story in this volume), when Sal has things in her purse to help her remember her day? Sometimes a special rock, shell, or other memento can bring an entire adventure, trip or vacation back to our memory.

Ezra Jack Keats has written many other wonderful books. Your child will enjoy *Peter's Chair*, and *The Pet Store*, and *Apartment 3* among others.

 # THE QUIET WAY HOME

Title: *The Quiet Way Home*
Author: Bonny Becker
Illustrator: Benrei Huang
Copyright: 1995

Summary

A grandfather and granddaughter take the road less traveled and delight in small sounds, too good to miss.

Bible

The man and child in *The Quiet Way Home* decide to turn away from the frantic noises of life and have a delightful time noticing the very small noises of the more private path. This is a wonderful reminder to pull back from the rush of living and come to a place of quiet and peace. Quiet is a state of repose and calm and it *can* be a place of refreshment and renewal. Knowing how to quiet down is important in being able to hear God. His call to us to be still and cease striving, is found in Psalm 46:10 (check different versions). Getting a new perspective and enjoying the small wonders of life, is an important habit to develop. Encourage your child by leading the way, and finding some small things to ponder and appreciate. This quiet time together can make all the difference in a day. Psalm 131:2 speaks of quieting and composing our soul. Proverbs 17:1 says a little with quietness is better than lots with strife. And 1 Peter 3:4 talks about the important quality of a gentle, quiet spirit, which is very precious in God's sight. A quiet or gentle answer that turns away anger is another important concept found in Proverbs 15:1. Choose one of these ideas. Say it aloud and then practice it often with your child.

Relationships

Talk about relationships. Relationships are how people relate to each other. We relate to family members, friends, and others acquaintances who help us in certain ways, like a grocer or bus driver, etc. With your child, name some different relationships such as mother and child, brother and sister, aunts or grandparents, friends, cousins, etc. How many kinds of relationships might be found in the double-sided title page picture? Mother and children, father and children, friends, brothers and sisters, teachers and children, bus driver and children, etc. As you read and study different books, magazines, etc., keep looking for examples of relationships and point out a new one now and then.

Art

Finding the beginning. One day, after you have read *The Quiet Way Home*, try to find the beginning of this story. Where does the book actually begin? The beginning of the story, by way of the *illustrations*, is on the title page where school lets out. So, the story begins *before* the text. This will be mildly interesting to your young child, but your older child might be intrigued by this "picture beginning" to the story, since it is an unusual occurrence. He may want to draw pictures and write a story in this manner.

Colors

On the right side of the title page there are three cars. Name the colors. Red, yellow and blue are primary colors. If you would like, give your child only these three tins of watercolor paint. You can pop out the other tins of paint from a Prang® color box and save them. Using just the red, yellow and blue, let your child paint some designs or

pictures of his own. See if he makes his *own* discovery that red and yellow blend into orange, blue and yellow into green, and blue and red into violet. Of course you *can* teach these principles, but a child's own discoveries are such a triumph! These personal discoveries are so special that they are almost never forgotten. Teachers can always try to present information in a way that allows children to make their own "discoveries."

Balance

Young children are often introduced to the idea of balance as they play on a teeter-totter (see-saw). They can also learn that balance is a part of many things around them. Very young children learn balance in order to walk. Older children learn to balance themselves on a two-wheeled bicycle. Balance is also a part of the world of art. For your older child, you can introduce the concept of balance in architecture by looking at the picture of the school on the title page. Ask your child to point to the large door in the middle of the school. Notice that there are two smaller doors; one on each side. This is a balanced or *symmetric* design. There is also a window on each side of the large middle door, a window over each of the smaller doors and an even number of windows over the middle door, each of which provide a balancing statement. Look for examples of balanced architecture as you go on outings, and conversely, notice buildings that have an *asymmetric* or unbalanced design. Bring up additional applications of balance, both physical and artistic, as you see the opportunity.

Math

After an enjoyable reading of the story, count the illustrations of daisies in the field. Count the number of quiet noises that the grandfather and child heard or made. Count the number of cars throughout the story or the total number of vehicles of all kinds.

Science: Human Body

This story is concerned with hearing and would present an opportunity to discuss "ears" and how they work. Mention the outer ear and how it gathers sound. Cup your hands and place them behind your ears. Can you hear even more? Now cover your ears with your hands. Did things just get quieter? Discuss loud noises and the fact that some noises can actually harm our hearing. Name some loud noises. Name some quiet noises and wonder over the fact that there are some sounds too soft for people to hear. Talk about voice descriptions, like whispers, shouts, murmurings, exclamations, guffaws, chortles, etc. Sing in a loud voice and then in a soft voice. Beat a drum loudly and then softly. Think of other loud and soft activities. Where would there be a quiet place near your home?

Health

For an active afternoon of exercise, read the story and then take turns acting out all the various activities you see in the illustrations; playing catch, hopscotch, dumping the trash cans, trying to hold back an angry dog, skipping, jumping, waving, knocking, hugging, pushing, etc. One of you could perform an action and let the other try to guess it. Then, when appropriate, take a walk in a quiet place, and listen to all the softer noises that would have been obscured in a place with more noise.

In this story, the grandfather and child sit in a field of dandelions. It seems amazing that they actually appreciate this vast display of "fairy tale-like" seed puffs. Indeed, there is quiet beauty in the yellow blossom, as well as in the miracle of a circlet of tiny seed parachutes. If you can, take a moment to find a dandelion and enjoy holding a yellow blossom under each other's chin to see the yellow reflection. (An old children's game originating with buttercups was to ask, "Do you like butter? Let's see!" and then hold a bright, yellow dandelion beneath a child's chin. When the child's chin glowed a rich, buttery yellow the "tester" would reply, "Yes, you *do* like butter!") Spend several minutes examining the beauty of the white seed head and then PUFF! watch them fly. Make a chain of dandelions to put around your child's neck. Now, make one for *you*, too.

In the field of dandelions, the story characters hear a grasshopper, which allows you to bring up the subject of insects. Take some time to look for insects with your child. What other insects are noted for their noises? Buzzing bees or flies, whining mosquitoes, chirping crickets, loud thrumming cicadas, clicking beetles, etc. It is fun learning about these insects, but even more fun when you hear one!

Make a List

Continuing the science lesson on hearing, you could begin a list of all the quiet things you and your child can *imagine*, like wind in the grass, or fluffy towels being folded, or raindrops hitting soft mud, etc. Also, the list can be of *actual* things. So your child might include specifically on the list: "The gentle ticking of the round clock in the hall," while the kitchen clock might be one that ticks quite loudly. Have fun with the list. Add to it regularly. Keep it up all year if you can. As you add to it now and then, when something occurs to you that is a quiet sound, you and your child will discover the vast variety of quiet sounding things that never could have been listed or thought of all at once. This type of exercise keeps your child aware of the sound of things around him, increasing his skill of observation.

Details

Your young child might like a "See If You Can Find It" exercise. After reading the story, ask him if he can find the bird's nest in the tree, blackbirds on a telephone wire, a parking meter, a cat with only his ears and tail showing (no face or paws), a wooden fence (there is a white one and a brown one), an iron fence, the American flag, and a jump rope. Keep it fun. If he's tired of searching, don't ask any more. Some children enjoy this kind of "I Spy" game more than others. For a super child detective, ask if he can find the three places where the girl is *not* wearing her backpack.

If he is interested in writing and drawing, your child might like to make his *own* book someday. He can begin to anticipate that "someday" project even at this young age by beginning to notice details that he might want to use later. After you have read the story and your child has seen the pictures, ask him if he noticed the variety of clothing, patterns and textures the characters are wearing: striped pants, dotted and checked shirts, patterned dresses, different hats, shoes and backpacks. There is such a variety from which to choose! Again, the life skill encouraged here is observation. Learning to be observant has many positive applications. You will probably notice your child's increased awareness of details as he looks at characters in books and then notices the wonderful variety of clothing styles of the people around him. Help your child learn to *appreciate* variety in styles at a young age. This sense of appreciation may help him avoid the all-too-common spirit of ridicule that often happens when children see something or someone unusual.

PLAY WITH ME

Title: *Play With Me*
Author: Marie Hall Ets
Illustrator: Marie Hall Ets
Copyright: 1976

Summary

How does one learn to appreciate wild things? Can they be approached in the same way as everything else?

Bible

One Bible lesson that might fit with this story is the Genesis creation narrative of Adam naming the animals. Other Bible verses on quietness from the preceding lesson of *The Quiet Way Home* page 65, might be fit here, also.

Art

Does your child like these illustrations? The sketch marks are so simple and yet there is personality in the girl and many of the animals. In each picture, only the girl and the creature she is pursuing are rendered in color. Why do you think the illustrator did this? Maybe she wanted to make them stand out and be the focal point of each page. Also, as the story progresses, you can see more animals and thus more color growing with each turn of the page. The one exception is the blue jay. Do you wish he had been blue?

Emotions

After reading the story, go back with your child and note the emotions on the face of the girl. The first picture is one of anticipation. You could ask your child, "What do you think the girl is feeling as she goes to play?" Or, "Does she look like she's excited about her time to play in the meadow?"

Follow the girl's changing moods as the story progresses. First notice her look of interest and wonder, then her moment of sadness as she watches the bug make trails on the water, her shivering quiet excitement as she waits quietly while the creatures come close to her, and finally the total eye-squinching happiness as she sits with animals that were no longer afraid. After turning the last page of text in the story, there is a picture. This illustration shows the end result of the wonderful discovery of sitting quiet and still in the midst of nature. The fruit of the girl's patience and stillness is portrayed by the large smiling sun and the high stepping girl—joy! She has learned her lesson well and is full of ecstatic, energetic joy.

Science: Morning Dew

The little girl goes to the meadow to play when the sun is barely up and the dew is still on the grass. Some early summer morning, take your child outside—barefoot! If he comments on the fact that the grass is wet, you can let him know that the wetness is called *dew*. This is a simple, tangible exercise in vocabulary building. Your three-year-old does not have to know how dew forms. That will come in the lessons of later years. But an outing with you, wet feet and a new word to ponder create an excitement about learning. There's nothing quite like hearing your child exclaiming to his dad or grandma, "I got my feet wet in the *dew* this morning!"

Science:

Make an animal card for your classification game for any new creatures in this story. Where did each animal hide in the meadow? The grasshopper sat on leaves of plants and ate them. The frog was close to the pond chasing mosquitoes. The turtle was sunning on the end of a log in the pond. The chipmunk was at an oak tree eating acorns, while the blue jay flew through trees on the meadow's edge. The rabbit was nibbling a flower, but ran into the woods, and the snake moved through the grass and down his hole.

Take a walk in a meadow or field and find a safe place to sit quietly (watch out for poison ivy!). The longer you sit, the more you and your child will notice. An excellent exercise in self-control (like learning to sit quietly) is to go to the same spot for a brief time each day. Maybe you can sit quietly three minutes the first day, five minutes the second and so on, building the habit of self-control. By going to the same place, you will also begin to notice things you didn't see on previous visits. Keep a record of what you see and read it back to your child at the end of a week or two.

Since wildlife is *wild*, animals and insects are more easily watched and appreciated than made into playmates. Take time often to quietly watch and enjoy the wide variety of plant and animal life around you. Then your child will experience the exhilaration of the little girl shown in the illustration which follows page 31!

Science: Pond Life and Experiencing Nature

Visit a pond. Take a walk around it. Listen for the "eek-plop" of frogs as they jump from the bank to the water when you get too near. Look for signs of insects, turtles, fish and water birds.

Other animal life is mentioned in the story. There is a blue jay, chipmunk, rabbit, snake and a fawn. Sometime when you and your child are outside, (if you are able) point out a blue jay and say, "Look! There's a blue jay like we read about in our story!" You may be able to point out a rabbit or chipmunk. If you do not live in a rural setting, pet stores often carry snakes and a zoo might have a fawn. Plan a short field trip and let your young child personally experience some of the things that he reads about in books. This provides memorable learning opportunities and gives him a chance to *compare* his experience to the material he has read about in books.

Literature

Play With Me is a book about nature. Another wonderful book about nature is *My Big Book of the Outdoors*, written by Jane Werner Watson and beautifully illustrated by Eloise Wilkin, 1983, Goldencraft. It is out of print at this time, but you could order it from your library or look for it at thrift shops and used book sales. It is worth the search. Watson's delightful book opens up the wonders of nature for your young child with pictures that he will remember forever.

Details

Noticing details is a part of becoming more observant. After reading the story, ask your child to name the color of the little girl's eyes. If he has trouble finding the answer to the question, let him know it was kind of a *trick question* because the only place you can see the color of her eyes is on the *cover*! This begins to teach that there are special pictures and details worth noticing throughout a good book—including the covers, flyleaves, table of contents, etc.

Emotions

The plaintive words of the little girl that no one would play with her tugs at our heart strings and reminds us of our own times of loneliness. *Everyone* has been lonely at one time or another. Everyone has wished for company. For some, it might be the company of family or friends, while others long for the company of a special pet or the enjoyment of the company of wild creatures. Ask your child if he has ever felt this emotion. What did he do? When we have problems we can either complain and become angry, or we can do whatever it takes to correct the problem. Once again, patience and quietness is often a help in sorting out the problem. Share with your child specific memories you might have in the area of loneliness. If he has not personally experienced loneliness, reading *Play With Me* will begin to expose him to this very real emotion. Perhaps your child will notice someone else who is lonely and have compassion for *him*. Do you know someone suffering from loneliness that you and your child could go visit? Perhaps a grandparent, widow, neighbor, former teacher, aunt or uncle. Read the story *Benjamin in the Woods* by Eleanor Clymer to empathize with a child in need of a friend.

Language Arts

Before reading the story again, ask your older child to be listening for the little girl's name. Ask, "Does the author tell us the little girl's name?" After the reading, discuss the fact that the author never tells. The little girl in the book is telling the story herself and she never tells her name. Is this surprising for your child? Authors sometimes leave little *mysteries* for their readers.

Nature: Close Up

One way to bring nature close enough for your child to examine is to feed the birds. There are ready-made birdfeeders for sale and a wide variety of wonderful patterns for creating your own special birdfeeders. State Conservation departments often have large, colorful posters of various native bird species. Often, these posters are free. Your child will love feeding the birds and delight in the opportunity to take a closer look at nature!

Music

Read *Play With Me* and when you're finished, thank the Lord for the magnificent world He created. Sing a hymn such as "This is My Father's World," "For the Beauty of the Earth" or other songs praising God for His creation. Even though your very young child may be unable to sing along, he will enjoy the sound of your voice and catch a phrase or two. Make up simple songs together that thank God for birds, trees, etc.

PRAYER FOR A CHILD

Title: *Prayer For A Child*
Author: Rachel Field
Illustrator: Elizabeth Orton Jones
Copyright: 1941
Award: Caldecott Medal

Summary

A prayer offered by a child is full of warmth and faith.

Bible

There are many verses on the subject of prayer. Continuing the book's theme of "blessing," Numbers 6:24 is familiar verse. Psalm 67 is another good passage to read in connection with this story. In Matthew 14:19 Jesus blesses the loaves and fishes.

Food

Read the story together. Then, as you talk about the different things that the young girl is asking God to bless, discuss the bread and milk. These are very basic, wholesome foods. Ask your child if he knows where you get milk. If he says, "the store," ask him where the store gets their milk. Eventually, he will discover that milk comes from cows and you can discuss dairy farms, how the cows are milked and how the milk is stored in chilled tanks and then pumped into milk trucks to be taken to the dairies, etc.

Follow the same discussion route with the bread, asking how your child thinks bread is made. Talk about fields of wheat and *show* him some wheat if you can. Discuss the grinding process and adding water and other ingredients to the flour. Talk about the baking process. You may want to talk about bakeries and delivery trucks. When your child thanks God for his bread and milk and asks the Lord to bless them, he may also want to ask a blessing on all the people involved in getting the bread and milk to his house.

Fears

After an enjoyable reading of this book, talk about the subject of fears. The prayer for quiet and restful sleep and freedom from frightening things is important for young children. Knowing that other children (and adults) have prayed the same prayers and felt the same feelings, helps diffuse the anxiety. Your child then begins to build faith that the Lord will see him through.

Contentment

One of the quiet wonders of this story is the contentment displayed by the girl as she appreciates each familiar thing around her and asks the Lord's blessing upon it. There is not the impatient yearning for more and more things, but rather a solid thankfulness for what she has. Exclaim over how thankful she is and what a wonderful character that shows. Turn to the picture opposite the text, "Bless the lamplight, bless the fire." Draw your child's attention to the girl who has paused in her reading to simply appreciate the most basic, familiar things around her. Look also at the picture opposite, "So, let me sleep and let me wake...," and notice the total peace and contentment on her face. Read this story often with your child and develop the habit of looking around from time to time and calling his attention to certain special small things for which you can give thanks together. Let him see

you be content and happy with the things you have. As he sees the peace on your face, he will be learning by example.

Geography and Culture

After reading the book, go back with your child to the page with the text, "Bless other children, far and near..." and look at the picture. Enjoy with him the variety of dress and face types of these children and show him a map or globe. Talk about children living in many places around the world. Based on the clothes, some of these children must live where it is cold and some must live where it is warm. When you're out shopping, notice people wearing unique clothing styles from foreign lands. Also look in magazines, books, and examine dolls in toy stores for other examples. Help him learn to enjoy the variety of culture. These exercises help your child develop a tolerance of others. He becomes interested and excited about the world around him. What a wonderful time to introduce the song, "Jesus Loves the Little Children."

Language

After reading the story, turn to the last page and discuss the word, "Amen." It means *let it be so*. The relaxed, peaceful, sleep of the little girl in the picture demonstrates her faith that God has heard her prayer. She clearly believes that whatever happens, God will care for her.

Rhyme

This story is a series of rhyming couplets. Your young child does not need to know this now, but the reading and rereading of this story will begin to instill a love of verse that can last a lifetime. You might just ask him if he likes the sounds of the words as you read the story. He will find out someday that a poet chooses words carefully that sound good together, to give the poem a special emotional punch. Poetry is something you hear as well as read—even if you read it silently. The reader experiences and enjoys poetry in a different way than he responds to prose.

Art

One of the most interesting parts of the beautiful illustrations is the wooden figurines. They are visible from the title page to the ending, and on each page in-between. Examine them carefully and ask your child what each one is doing. Has your child ever seen any figures that remind him of these? He might have seen Hummel® figures, or carved wooden figures from a Noah's Ark set or a Christmas nativity set. Now and then, look in gift shop windows with him and see if you can find any sculptures that remind you of Elizabeth Orton Jones' beautiful wooden figures.

The rest of the pictures are exquisite in details and just re-examining the prayer by looking together at the illustrations *only* will yield many moments of surprise finds! Make a game of it. Find something that interests you, like the inside fabric of the pillow cover in the last picture. Then, ask your child to find something *he* thinks is interesting.

Recognizing Similarities and Differences In Pictures

If you have an especially observant child who loves details, examine the first picture of the girl on her "soft and waiting bed," about the sixth page. Look at the picture carefully. Then, turn to the last large picture in the book preceding the "Amen." Can your child remember things that are the same in these pictures? Is there anything different or added in the last picture? (The girl is *in* bed rather than *on* it and she is holding a stuffed bear that did not appear in the first picture. You can also see the colorful fabric under the pillowcase.)

Another picture you might want to explore is the view of the child as she asks the Lord's blessing on her milk and bread. Point out the shiny cup and the slice of bread. Notice the tablecloth. Then look for the picture of the little girl opposite the words "So let me sleep and let me wake in peace and health for Jesus' sake." What is different about *this* picture? (The mug is empty and the bread is gone.) Now, ask your child, "what are some of the things that are the same in these two pictures?" (The little girl has the same clothes and the same bow in her hair. The tablecloth is also the same.)

Project

Go through the book's illustrations together with your child, notice how many times a button or buttons appear in the pictures. Take a shoestring and string buttons from an old button box. You and your child can sort them first by number of holes, then by color, then by size, etc. See who can make the longest string.

Science

The phrase, "Through the darkness, through the night," is opposite a picture with stars visible through the window. Stargazing is a wonderful way to enjoy the immensity of God's creation, encourage a sense of wonder in your child, and spend special time together. Snuggling up close and just pointing at different pretty stars is making a memory. In later years, your child may enjoy learning some of the names of the more familiar star groups. Lay the foundation now!

Literature

Another book that you might enjoy is *Prayers for Children* with pictures by Eloise Wilkin, 1952, 1974 Western Publishing Co. It is a Little Golden Book. The prayers and the illustrations are memorable!

I AM AN ARTIST

Title: *I Am an Artist*
Author: Pat Lowery Collins
Illustrator: Robin Brickman
Copyright: 1992

Summary

The world is overflowing with examples of art that even the young can see!

Bible

The Lord is the *original* artist. He has created a world full of beauty, intricacy and magnificence. Pat Lowery Collins has written a book encouraging young people to take part in the artistic experience by appreciating the great works of the Lord and all the places art can be found. Isaiah 6:3b says to comprehend that the entire earth is full of God's glory. Other verses like Psalm 19:1 say that the heavens proclaim the glory of God.

Whether you are considering the sun, a rainbow, beautiful clouds, moon, stars or planets, the heavens do declare the glory of God! If you have not already introduced the creation story itself, you might find this a good opportunity.

Science: Nature

The entire *I Am an Artist* narrative is concerned with nature, and finding the correlation between art and nature. In this book, you have an opportunity to discuss leaves, caterpillars, clouds, shells, feathers, salamanders, and countless other aspects of nature. Whenever possible, experience *with* your child the actual objects and views. Watch a sunset together and see how the colors change from one to another until the light is gone. One day when you read the story, have a sand dollar shell (like the round white one on the cover of the book) so your child can see the designs and feel the texture. While on a walk, pick up a feather and examine it with your child.

Go to a pet store and watch the salamanders and an abundant variety of God's other works of art. Find a rough stone and a polished stone (you might have to purchase the polished stone), and let your child look at them and *feel* the difference. Do you have a horseshoe crab shell like the one on the back cover? Maybe you could find one at a shell shop or nature store, or borrow one from a friend for a few days. On different days when you read the book, bring out various objects as a surprise and watch your child's interest and wonder grow. Look for a rainbow, a sunrise or sunset, a bank of beautiful clouds, or watch for a falling star and enjoy it together. Have fun twirling a hose around and watching the arcs and spirals of water. Then stare at a drop of water and see if you notice a reflection of what is around you. Look for shapes, patterns, textures and colors and try imitating some the shapes and colors with pencils or crayons, or paint on paper.

Math

There are many objects in Collins' book to count. You could count the pine tree trunks, the stars, other nature objects, etc. Or you could use this book as a basis for making counting flash cards with nature objects to count, match, or use in playing the memory game. (While you can readily buy "memory game" cards at a store, these games are often more fun if you make them yourself and tie them to a favorite story.)

For your older child, there is also an opportunity to use actual stones, shells, beans, etc., as math aids for a simple introduction to counting, adding and subtracting. This brings variety, inspiration and fun into math and sets a positive stage for later learning.

Science: Environments

Discuss the different places that plants and animals are found. Some live in or around oceans, lakes, ponds, or streams. Some live in forests, deserts, mountains, etc. One or several of these places could be discussed. Enrich your discussion by finding *very simple* library books on the topic.

Science: Senses

Talk about the five senses: sight, touch, hearing, smell, and taste. All of the senses are used as we observe the rich variety of nature and nature's art. Focusing on touch, look at the title page—the first page inside the cover of the book. This page has a picture of a feather. The feather looks *soft* to the touch, although some feathers can be *stiff*. There is also a picture of a shell with a *sharp* point, and a transparent cicada wing that is so *fragile*. The leaf looks rather *crunchy*, while the flower pod seems as if it would be *smooth*.

There is such a variety of things to notice in nature with our noses: the smell of the rain before a storm or the irresistible smell of fresh mown hay. Nature is also filled with fascinating sounds: the wind in the trees, or the dried leaves rustling in the street. What is that funny chirping sound outside the door or the chorus of spring peepers after the first rain? Use Collins' book to begin an adventure in the world of nature as well as art, enjoying what the Lord has made and learning of His greatness.

Character

In this fast-paced world with too much to do, finding moments of quiet contemplation is often difficult. Can you guide your child in the habit of "taking time to smell the roses?" Being able to slow down and notice the minutia of nature in all its aspects is restorative in ways that are hard to understand. It is quieting for the soul, and leaves us inspired and fresh for the next task. Philippians 4:8 reminds us that we will do well to think on things that are lovely and worthy of praise. Looking for art in nature and enjoying creation itself with your child, are wonderful ways to fulfill this verse.

Science: Tracks

In the book *I Am an Artist*, you can see footprints in the snow on the page with the forest of pine trees. Like footprints, wildlife often makes tracks that people can discover and appreciate. Petite, hand-like footprints in the mud by a stream lets us know a raccoon has visited in the night. Many other types of tracks can be found in dust, sand, mud, or snow. Keep a look-out for tracks. Even at an early age, excitement over finding a track can create such an interest that skills of observation rapidly increase as your child is constantly looking for more evidence of animal life around him.

Art

This book introduces the concepts of *line, texture, color,* and *design*, as it is witnessed in nature. Find nature objects that have a line to follow, like the long stem of a leaf which can be traced to the end of each of the leaf's veins, or the spiraling line of a nautilus shell, etc. Let your child trace these lines with his finger. If he is interested, let him take a large-diameter pencil and make a similar line on paper until his paper is filled with a variety of lines.

Discuss *texture*, the appearance and feel of an object. While line defines a two dimensional shape, texture lets us see or feel the third dimension of depth. Let your child feel trees with rough bark and smooth bark, seed pods that are smooth or very rough, and rocks, leaves and other objects that have a variety of textures. You can continue this discussion with pieces of cloth of many varying textures, food that has definite differences in texture, etc. These "feeling" games are equally fun with your eyes closed. Have your child close his eyes and then one by one, hand him a variety of items with wildly differing textures. You can also put several items with different shapes and textures into a drawstring bag or old sock. Let your child reach down into the bag and feel various items without looking. Now see if he can identify the item from feel and texture only.

With your help, your child will slowly begin to understand the word *texture*, which at first is simply understood through the question "how does it feel?" As he begins to "see" the differences of texture in nature, he will be better prepared to learn techniques to "show" how texture looks in an object on paper when he is older. Artists draw what they know, and what they have experienced.

Straight Line

Curved Line

Spiral

Jagged Line

Broken Line

Even drawings of imaginary creatures or unvisited planets are made up from shapes, forms and textures that are familiar to the artist. Your child will be better prepared to express himself through art later, because of the experiences you're sharing together today. This story clearly suggests that *anyone* who "sees" lines, textures, etc., in nature is an artist!

ANGUS LOST

Title: *Angus Lost*
Author: Marjorie Flack
Illustrator: Marjorie Flack
Copyright: 1932

Summary

Curiosity gets the "dog" and leads him away from home.

Bible

Angus was lost and that is often frightening. But, the Lord is with us wherever we go, and He says not to be afraid because He is always with us. Talk with your child about what he should do if he becomes lost:

First: *He can remember that he is not alone, that God is with him.*

Second: *He should try to calm down.*

Third: *He should remember and follow your instructions for neighborhoods, malls, etc.*

This is the type of lesson that you can share calmly, reminding your child of these important lessons until he can repeat to you the three responses without a pause. Even then, you may still want to review these important concepts every now and then!

Character and Safety: Curiosity

Wondering about new and exciting things is a good attribute. Angus wondered what the world was like outside his own yard. However, curiosity needs some balance of wisdom. Discuss Angus' desire to see more of his world and the consequences in his story. Maybe your child has seen something he would like to explore. Let him know he can come to you, and you will go with him to see the thing that is exciting him. When you use a story like *Angus Lost* to begin a conversation on practicing "safe curiosity" the topic becomes enjoyable and memorable!

Sayings

"Curiosity killed the cat," is an old saying originating from the intensely curious nature of cats which gets them into precarious situations. The saying is mentioned here just as an interesting tid-bit. You can decide if it would appropriate to bring it up.

Also, at the end of the story, Angus was back at his very own home! He saw the same yard and the same house and the same cat. Talk about home and what makes it nice. Introduce the old phrases "Home, sweet home," and "There's no place like home!"

Language Arts: Possessives

When you walk or drive up to your home with your child, say, "This is <your child's name>'s home. For example: This is *Sam's* home. This is where *Sam* lives. This is *Sam's* dog, etc. Using this phraseology every now and then will lay a foundation in ownership. In later years, the concept of an apostrophe showing ownership or possession may be more easily understood.

Art

Go through the illustrations. Name the colors you see: blue, yellow, pink, green, black, orange, brown. Look at the picture of Angus coming out of the cave after the snow storm. Notice the snow with the blue shadows and the yellow and pink of the sky. If you live in an area that receives snow in the winter, keep watching for an early morning or late afternoon sky that reminds you of this picture. If you see one, say, "Look! Doesn't this sky remind you of the picture in *Angus Lost?*"

Look at the wheels on the milk wagon. Ask your child if they remind him of anything. They could look like a pie with the pieces already cut. The shape of each piece is called a *wedge*. And the wheel itself is a *circle*. If you happen to have baked a pie, you can ask your child, "Would you care for a *wedge* of pie?"

On another reading of the story, look for pictures with lots of action. Talk about the names for the actions: running, barking, baa-ing, butting, crawling, and waiting, etc.

Silhouette

Lay a foundation for later lessons on *silhouettes* (as an art technique). Do this by merely pointing out that some areas of the illustrations show details and color. For instance, in some pictures you can see Angus' fur and his pink collar. But, in other views of Angus, he looks as if he has been cut from a piece of black paper, with no detail or color at all. Just comment to your child that you find this interesting and wondered if he has noticed.

Science: Dogs and Dog Safety

Notice that in this story there are two dogs but they do not look the same. There are many different kinds of dogs. Show your child a book, poster or a page from an encyclopedia illustrating different breeds. Enjoy the wonder of such a wide and sometimes unusual variety. Your child will be eager to watch for interesting dogs in his neighborhood!

You may want to take this opportunity to discuss ways to behave around dogs, both familiar ones and ones that are strangers. Dogs do not generally like to be hit or used as a chair, horse, or step stool. Be careful whenever dogs are eating or chewing a bone. At these times they do not like to be disturbed. Often, if dogs are bothered during eating, they may growl or nip. Remember the old saying to "let sleeping dogs lie," and leave them alone while they nap. Be careful and don't reach through a fence toward a strange dog. He may bite! When you greet a new dog, extend a fisted hand and let the dog sniff it and become used to you. This approach can protect tender fingers if the dog becomes agitated. Remind your child that many dogs are friendly, but some are not!

Dog *care* is another topic of canine related information. Dogs need water and food. They need exercise. They enjoy kind, soft words and lots of love. They need a comfortable place to sleep. And, if they are quartered outside, perhaps a dog house to protect them from the elements. Most dogs receive yearly visits to the dog doctor (veterinarian) at which time they get vaccinations to prevent various diseases. Discuss any of these ideas with your child and remind him that it is good to be kind to animals.

Science: Milk

When Angus is lost he follows a horse-drawn cart home. This cart or wagon belongs to the milkman. Talk about the different ways milk used to be delivered, and about how we generally buy it in cartons at the store today. Find the picture of the milk wagon in *Angus Lost* and point to it. Ask your child, "Where did the milkman get the milk to put in his cart?" If he doesn't know, show him pictures of cows and explain briefly. How ever milk has been delivered or made store-ready, it has always come from cows (more rarely, goats). If he is interested, find a video of the milking process (just show a small portion) or take a field trip and see milking first hand. He won't understand all of the procedure, but it will help him to understand his world just a little better. The time spent together will be the best of all!

Animals

Watch the story for animals such as the goat, the owl, ducks and the cat. If you are playing the animal classification game, begun in the lessons *Blueberries for Sal,* make a card for any new animals.

Science: Caves
Simulate the Wonder of a Spelunking Expedition (or Cave Exploration):

Before You Begin...
The following suggestion is one that requires a great deal of time, energy and creativity. This project certainly isn't *mandatory*. Be sure to add ideas of your own to the directions! Remember that this same type of project can be used again and again to demonstrate many different learning situations.

First of all, find several (three or four) large boxes. (You could also use one of the fabric wrapped, coil-spring "tunnels" designed for children's play if you already have it.) Open the box ends so that one box can join another to make a long tunnel. Place one end of your "tunnel" under a large table or inside a large closet. Place a heavy blanket over the table to help make it dark inside. Or, plan your cave adventure after dark. If you use the closet idea, hang a dark drape from the top of the closet doorway over the end of the box to make the closet dark.

Next, gather some props. If you have a realistic rubber salamander, a furry stuffed toy bat, some clear plastic icicles from your Christmas decorations to mimic stalagmites and stalactites, use them. If not, find a picture of a salamander in an outdoor or nature magazine or draw and color one yourself. Do the same with the bat. Find

some clay and fashion some pretend stalagmites and stalactites. You could even have a shallow dish with some rocks that are damp for your child to feel.

Before you actually use the cave, spend some time talking about caves such as the one in which Angus spent the night. Find a very simple book on caves at your library and read it together. Last of all, pack a small snack and a plastic bottle of water to enjoy sometime during your cave exploration. Perhaps your child has a small backpack or belt-pack to carry his provisions. With these preparations accomplished, introduce your child to your "homemade cave".

The idea is to have your child crawl into the tunnel entrance and proceed till he comes to the cave. He may take a flashlight with him! You are to be under the table or in the closet to greet him. As he approaches the main cave entrance, have him switch off the flashlight and hand it to you. Help him into the area and sit together on the floor. Talk about the darkness. Tell him that when you turn on the light he will not see any green plants like grass or trees inside the cave. (Green plants must have light to live.) Does he like the darkness? (You can always tie in this exercise to *Angus Lost* by saying, "I wonder if the dark cave bothered Angus, or if *he* liked it?) Now ask your child what he might find in a cave. Let him know that caves often have dripping water and damp wet places. Let him touch the damp bowl of rocks. Now, say, "What else is in this cave?" Shine your flashlight on the spot with the salamander. Exclaim over this animal and talk about what it likes, such as out of the way damp places and insects that it finds near the cave. (Wonder aloud whether or not Angus saw a salamander, or if one hid from him.) Then ask again, "What else could be in this cave?" Now shine your light on the bat, hanging upside down from a high place. Talk about how they come out of the cave at night to eat many insects. Mention that they have special ability to fly in darkness without bumping into anything! (Angus may not have seen the bats leave if he was sleeping.) If you have something to represent the stalagmites and stalactites, shine your light on these and just say that they are interesting, that they are formed over many years by dripping water. If you haven't already had your snack, take time, enjoy your provisions and marvel at the wonder of caves. Turn the flashlight back off. Let your eyes try to adjust to the dark as you think about what you've seen. Then give your child the flashlight and let him crawl back through the tunnel.

For the most part, the entire cave project is just an avenue to have fun together. Any learning picked up along the way is fine, but not the primary goal here. As previously mentioned, there are many other scenarios that you could simulate in an enjoyable adventure experience together. (A space capsule, plane, train, boat, deep sea diving, sunken ship, covered wagon, gold mine, etc.)

If you have several young children, you might consider taking each of them into the cave on separate occasions. Not only can you spend special time with each one this way, but it would be interesting to hear them talk to each other about their adventures and the things that especially impressed each of them.

KATY NO-POCKET

Title: *Katy No-Pocket*
Author: Emmy Payne
Illustrator: H. A. Rey
Copyright   1944

Summary

Katy, a mother kangaroo who does not have a pocket, searches for a solution to her problem. This search produces a story which has long been a favorite with children.

Bible

After searching for a solution to her no-pocket problem, Katy finally meets the man with the apron full of pockets. He gladly gives her this apron, saying it will be easy for him to get another. This generosity reminds us of the Bible verse Deuteronomy 15:8, which encourages us to give freely, and generously lend to those who have needs. Also, 1 Timothy 6:18 tells us to be full of good works and willing to share. Katy, after she receives the man's kindness, perpetuates the generosity by giving rides to all the animal babies!

Science: Animals

Katy No-Pocket includes many animals. Your child may not yet recognize some of them. The list of animals includes: crocodiles, deer, opossum, skunk, raccoons, snails, ostriches, and lizards. Also, from the "bug" category: worms, spiders and dragonflies. If you are playing the classification game begun in the *Blueberries for Sal* lessons, make a card for each of the new animals. Don't worry at this point about the invertebrate "bug" category.

This story provides a chance to help your child appreciate how each animal has its own way of caring for its babies. Some mother animals carry their babies on their backs and some use their arms. Some babies have to walk while others learn to fly, etc.

After another reading one day, take time to talk about the animals which are the most interesting to *your* child. You may want to find some very simple books at your library on these animals of special interest. Share these with your child, either reading the books or perhaps looking only at some of the pictures.

If you keep it light and fun, you might want to mention where some of these animals live. Remember, you are merely introducing ideas to your child, not getting him ready for a quiz! Try using a sense of humor. Ask "Have you seen any crocodiles around here lately?" "No? Why not?" "These animals live in different areas (or in different countries)." "How about a kangaroo?" "Yes, we did see one at the zoo last week but actually kangaroos live in a country called Australia." Or, "I just haven't seen any monkeys lately in the trees, or lions either, for that matter!" Talk about the other animals in the story and if there is great interest, discuss their native habitat.

We've discussed zoos before, but this might be a good time to mention that zoos allow us to see animals that may not live near us. Zoo outings may bring up interesting questions about animals, as well as about far-away places.

H. A. Rey has written two best-loved books that would fit into the category of where animals live and another about the zoo. Your library or local bookstore probably has *Anybody at Home?* ISBN 0395070457 and *Feed the Animals*, ISBN 0395070635. What makes these books so unique and popular are the pages that fold in half way. Read the rhyming message that gives a clue to who might live there or who the zookeeper might be feeding. After guessing, your child can open the page and see if he was right! Even very young children love the rhyming sounds and the opening of the flap to reveal more picture. These are special books, loved by children for nearly fifty years. (There is also a set of four of these H. A. Rey books in a hanging bag that children love to carry. The ISBN for this item is 039528659X and it is called *Four Fold-Out Books in a Bag*.)

Memory

Play a memory game by naming the items that fall out of the workman's apron. The items include a saw, wrench, nails, hammer, drill, tape measure, pliers, etc. You can ask your child how many items he remembers after the first reading. As you read the story to him another time he may be looking for more items. At additional readings your child may be excited at how his memory improves.

You could also use the animals who ride in the apron for memory fun: snail, lizard, frog, bird, turtle, monkey, kitten, joey (baby kangaroo), opossum, squirrel, skunk, raccoon, and rabbit.

Project for Memories

Find or make an apron with many pockets for your young child. There can be a special place for pencils, crayons, safety scissors, a package of tissues, etc., or it can hold toy tools. Another idea is for a blue apron to hold stuffed animals and hang on the wall. A project like this will make the reading of this book extra special and create a tangible memory.

Kindness and Gratitude

The man was kind to Katy when she inquired about the apron. She also did not forget to say thank you. Discuss how both of these character traits help make a world that is nice to live in. Everyone won't always act this way, but when people are polite, our world is more pleasant. You won't always play with your child at playtime, but now and then when you happen to be invited to one of your child's tea parties, practice your pleases and thank yous and your child will soon be imitating you.

Science: Plants and Animals

Find the picture with the owl in his home in the tree. Talk about the owl and his tree home. Maybe you and your child will have a chance to see one someday. What other creature is living in this tree? (Spider) Take a walk and find a big interesting tree. Can you find any animals or insects which use the tree for their home? (You might see a squirrel, bird, insect, spider, etc.) Many other animals use trees for a home or resting place. Among them are the bear, opossum, raccoon or snake, etc.

Have fun looking at different kinds of trees. Notice different bark, leaves, nuts or berries, etc. Your child may be interested to know that all trees do not have the same bark, leaves, fruit, etc. Becoming aware of the immensity of God's creation is one of the wonders of life!

Social Studies

The story *Katy No-Pocket* provides another chance to mention cities and city life. Looking at the picture of Katy in the city, notice and discuss the variety of buildings, people, and animals. Look carefully for the animals in the various city pictures: birds, dogs, cat, cow, horse, etc. In the city nearest you, would you be likely to see a cow or horse? There is also a street light, a bus stop, fire hydrant (some people refer to these as fire plugs), and a window washer!

Numbers

If your child loves to count things, after reading the story, have him count the animals (either on one page or for the entire story.) Or you could go page by page and keep an animal count for each.

Mothers

Read *Katy No-Pocket* and talk about the fact that Katy's story focuses on a mother's search to have the best for her child. Mothers are generally like that! Talk about mothers. If your child has grandparents, remind him that the grandmothers were his parent's mother. Tell stories and your memories about these grandmothers who took care of

their children, especially times when they worked
hard to provide the best for them.

Habitat

After another reading of the story, draw your
child's attention to the first picture of *Katy No-
Pocket* with the wide open spaces and small
plants. Then look together at the double-page picture of the city. Discuss different habitats, such
as country living, city living, living in the woods
or desert, etc. Notice all the details of city life in
these pictures: tall buildings with fire escapes,
street lights, buses, cars (one is a convertible),
trucks, bicycles, baby carriages, and a scooter, as
well as many people and pets. If you live in a
small town or in the country, make a special trip
to show your child a big city! He will see many of
the things you discussed in this lesson.

There is additional discussion that can take place
regarding the habitat of the various animals.
Some live in or near the water. Some live in trees.
Where does the owl live? (He lives in the hole of
an old dead tree.) Maybe you will see an owl on
an outing some day.

Numbers

You can help your child count all the animals in
this story, or as many as he can. You can also
draw simple pictures of these animals. Have your
older child make a tally mark under each picture
as you read the story. Then have him count his
marks.

WE'RE GOING ON A BEAR HUNT

Title   *We're Going On A Bear Hunt*
Author   Michael Rosen
Illustrated   Helen Oxenbury
Copyright   1989

Summary

This is an active story for fun loving children. A family goes on a bear hunt and finds more than it bargained for.

Bible

We're Going On A Bear Hunt is the story of a family on a journey. They travel through a meadow's deep grass, cross a cold river, slug through oozy mud, stumble into a dark forest, brave a snowstorm and investigate a cave. This is reminiscent of other families that took journeys in the Bible. Briefly tell about the Hebrews leaving Egypt, crossing the Red Sea and journeying in the desert before reaching the land that God had promised them. Another story of family travel is the time Jesus went with his family to Jerusalem. Talk about the things that they might have experienced on the way.

Drama

Act out the story *We're Going On A Bear Hunt*. There are many actions and expressions that would be fun to assume as you act out this story together.

At another time, you could name an action and let your child carefully turn the pages until he finds an example. Skipping, carrying or riding piggyback and holding a stick are pictured on the cover. Other actions include pulling or tugging, wading, huddling, throwing, pointing, hugging, tripping, climbing stairs and shutting the door.

Experiencing a Story

The family in *We're Going On A Bear Hunt* finds themselves squelching through oozy mud. Find a place to make a mud puddle. Let your child wiggle his toes in it. While he does recite the famous line of poetry, "Nobody else but the rose bush knows how good mud feels between the toes!"

Art: Illustrations

Notice the illustrations on both inside book covers. (There are two sets of pictures: one set on the front inside cover and a second set on the back inside cover.) Can your child point out the cave in both of these pictures? What is the difference between these two pictures? (One is in the sunlight during the day and the other is in the moonlight at night. Make it a point to view a certain scene outside your home in the daytime and again that night after dark. Remind your child how this is like the cave scenes in the story.

At another reading, enjoy some more of the illustrations. Pause over them and find more and more details in each illustration. Talk about the pictures. Find the flock of birds. You can say, "Look at the flock of birds. I didn't notice them before, did you? Where do you think they are going?" Can you find the house behind the hill? Notice the footprints in the snow. In the picture where the dog meets the bear, which do you think looks more surprised?

Comprehension

Here are some questions to chat about with your child after a reading of the story. In the picture with the words "splash splosh," the father and the children are carrying their shoes—why would they do this? (So they don't get their shoes wet. Wet shoes usually hurt your feet when you walk. Sometimes they rub and cause blisters and in general they are unpleasant.) Why does the baby still have *his* shoes on? (His shoes are still on because he is being carried.) Why does the father carry the baby? (He carries him because the water would be too deep for the baby to walk through.)

Relationships: Family

The family in *We're Going On A Bear Hunt* consists of a father and his four children. This family also has a pet dog. Families come in many sizes and varieties. If your child is old enough to understand, talk about different families that you know and perhaps draw the members of each family. Do these families have any pets?

Music

For those musically inclined, there is music in this story in the rhythms and repetitions of the words and actions. If you or your child wishes, try making up a song that tells the story of the *Bear Hunt*. First, there could be a slow plodding melody (through the mud). Then a light, airy melody (through he grasses) followed by an excited, agitated melody during the race back to the house, etc. If you are a musician, you could compose an instrumental piece as explained in the previous sentence. Then let your child guess what is happening in each different part of your composition. You could dedicate the piece to him, saying "I composed some music for you!"

THE RED CARPET

Title: *The Red Carpet*
Author: Rex Parkin
Illustrator: Rex Parkin
Copyright: 1948

Summary

Follow the runaway red carpet for a hilarious adventure.

Bible

The Duke was wonderfully pleased at his red carpet reception! He said the warm greeting filled him with cheer. Hebrews 13:2a says not to forget to show hospitality to strangers and Romans 12:13b reminds us to practice hospitality. As you put these verses into practice perhaps you and your child can make someone else feel as happy as the Duke!

Object Recognition

As each line is read on page one have your child point to objects as you mention them. You might ask him to search for a street sign, green window boxes, striped awnings, a doorman dressed in blue, and red carpet. Ask him to name other things in the picture: pink balloon, green purse, spotted dog, red hat, etc.

Sayings

The Duke in this story was a very important visitor. He received special treatment. Many times government diplomats and other officials receive special welcoming and hospitality treatments. Your older child may be interested in this idea, while your younger child will probably not understand. Regardless of age, however, they can begin to understand that sometimes people receive *special treatment*. With your child, plan a "You Are Special" occasion for someone. Maybe it is Daddy when he comes home from work. If you have some red material, have your child help you spread it on the floor. Greet him at the door with a homemade "You Are Special!" button and the explanation of the "red carpet" treatment. Lots of hugs and kisses are good, too. Then, serve a special dinner you have planned. This can be done for another relative, sibling, or friend as well. Your child will long remember the event and probably never forget the meaning of "the red carpet treatment."

Action

After you've read the story, look again at the pictures and follow and enjoy the action of the red carpet unrolling and rolling along. Notice the effects this wild carpet has on the people of the town!! How do they show their reaction? Can you or your child imitate them?

Vocabulary

A telegram is a message sent over telegraph wires. Explain this vocabulary word only if your child shows interest. The concepts are difficult and he has plenty of years to learn about telegraph messages.

CORDUROY

Title: *Corduroy*
Author: Don Freeman
Illustrator: Don Freeman
Copyright: Picture Puffin

Summary

A little girl wants a bear and a bear is looking for a friend.

Bible

Corduroy is looking for a friend. He finds a good friend in Lisa. Read Proverbs 17:17 and talk with your older child about what makes a good friend.

Manners

When Lisa's mother does not buy Corduroy for her and says it's time to go, Lisa leaves quietly, even though she wants the bear so much.

Sometime later, when Lisa returns home, she checks her piggy bank and finds she has enough money to buy Corduroy. She asks her mother again and her mother says she can buy the bear. Lisa is respectful, patient and kind to her mother.

Lisa is also respectful to the saleslady at the store when she buys Corduroy. The saleslady asks Lisa if she wants the bear in a box to take home. Lisa replies politely, "Oh, no thank you." Talk about *and* practice good manners—both at home *and* away from home. Remember to compliment your child whenever you witness examples of his polite and gracious manners.

Homes and Habitats

Corduroy wants a friend and a home. Talk about loving each other and having a home. Discuss what makes a family and a home. Give thanks to the Lord for such blessings.

Think together about the different kinds of places that people live. They may live in houses, apartments, mobile homes, motor homes, house boats, nursing homes, orphanages, space stations, submarines, tents, igloos, etc.

Animals

In the illustrations of *Corduroy*, you can find a giraffe, horse, turtle and a lion. If you are continuing the animal classification game begun in the lesson plans for *Blueberries for Sal*, add any additional animals you have found.

Science

When Corduroy first sees an escalator (pages 12-13), he mistakes it for a mountain. It is normal and easy to make mistakes when we haven't seen something before. Talk about this idea and possibly add an anecdote about a "mixed-up" experience you might have had. These conversations help your child understand that everyone makes some mistakes. He should not become overly embarrassed when he doesn't understand something. This will set the stage for enjoyable learning experiences. **Note:** A delightful "mix-up" story is "Little Brown Bear's Surprise" found in *The Merry Adventures of Little Brown Bear* by Elizabeth Upham. If you're not already familiar with these wonderful stories, locate a copy at your library and share them with your child!

If your child has never seen a real escalator, make plans to visit a building that has one and ride up and down with him.

Social Studies: Saving

Lisa sees Corduroy in a department store and wants to have him. Her mother tells her, "not today, I've already spent too much." Lisa quietly goes home. But, later the story says Lisa checks her piggy bank, has enough to buy the bear, and her mother gives her permission. Ask your child if he knows what a piggy bank is. Talk about savings banks and saving for things that you might want. Let your child make a special box or tin with a slot and give them coins now and then to save. Keep it fun and saving will become a habit!

Art

Look through the story illustrations with your child. Try to find the one you think has the most action. For instance, the action grows from looking (page 9), climbing down (page 10), and tugging (page 17), to where Corduroy flies backwards off the bed (page 18)! There is also running (page 29), sewing (page 31) and hugging (page 32). Act out some of these action words.

Art Project to Make a Memory

Some pattern companies have patterns that correspond to characters in children's books. If you desire, check several pattern catalogs to see if there is a pattern to make Corduroy as a surprise for your child. Or take a similar toy bear and make some green overalls with a missing button!

Another idea is to focus on buttons. Corduroy is so concerned because he has lost one of his buttons. Talk about buttons. What do buttons do? Did your child know that there are a great variety of buttons? If you (or a grandmother or great-grandmother) have an old button box full of interesting old buttons, get it out and have fun examining them. Perhaps your child would enjoy grouping the ones that are the same. You can also group them according to number of holes, color or size.

Games

Sometime when your family is gathered together, mention Corduroy and his all-important button and suggest playing "Button, Button Who Has the Button?" Hold a button between your clasped hands. As you stand inside a circle of people pretend to drop the button into each of their clasped hands. At some point you actually *do* deposit the button into someone's hands and continue for awhile so no one can tell who actually has it. Then someone tries to guess the new button holder.

Numbers
Count the beds and lamps on pages 14-15.

Re-Defining A Story
Tell a story using *Corduroy* as a *pattern*. Perhaps there is a boy (include an interesting description in your story) who has been wanting an animal or a fire truck, etc. He is told he cannot have it. He asks later if he can buy it for himself, etc. Make up an interesting story to go along with this scenario. Your child will be intrigued with hearing the same type of story but with different characters and possible outcome. He may want to make up an ending for the story himself! These types of interaction are valuable as creative thinking skills and learning to love stories and storytelling.

Literature
Corduroy, as well as all the *Before Five in a Row* titles, chronicles the activities of children. Children are busy. This busyness is their "work" and the play activities in which they engage help them to grow in many ways. Gyo Fujikawa has captured the world of childhood in a delightful book called, *Oh, What a Busy Day!* It is currently out of print but perhaps it will be reprinted soon. Until then, find it at your library. This book with its delightfully active illustrations will provide hours and hours of enjoyment for you and your child!

JENNY'S SURPRISE SUMMER

Title: *Jenny's Surprise Summer*
Author: Eugenie
Illustrator: Eugenie
Copyright: Golden Book

Summary

Jenny has to make a difficult decision. How will she decide?

Parent's Note

This book is currently out of print. It was included as an *extra title* because it provides an excellent opportunity to present decision making at a very young level. You may be able to find it at your library or from someone who has a collection of Golden Books. Not everyone will be able to locate this wonderful book, but if you are able to find it you will enjoy this special story.

Bible

Jenny's Surprise Summer presents a chance to talk about the verse in James 1:5 that explains how to ask for wisdom. Jenny needs wisdom to make her decision, and it is good for your child to know that when he has a decision to make he can rely on James 1:5. Two other verses that might be appropriate in the context of this story are Philippians 4:1 and Hebrews 13:5. These verses speak of being content with what you have. Jenny needs to become content with the idea of taking only one kitten home. Again, it is good for a child to know that the Lord will help him be content with what he has.

Vacations

This story provides a wonderful opportunity to discuss the subject of vacations and the places where people go: the mountains, the ocean, the lake, the desert, the woods, the country, the city, etc. Has your family been on a vacation? Have you ever had a special vacation when you were young? Share some of your memories. Do you have pictures or home movies that you could show your child?

Science

Explore the subject of ocean environments if your child is interested. You could talk about beaches, sand, salt water, shells, gulls, etc.

Science: Weather

In this story there is a thunderstorm. It comes up suddenly and rains hard. When you experience a heavy summer thunderstorm, remind your child of *Jenny's Surprise Summer* and how she hides in a cave till the storm is over. (Caves are discussed in *Angus Lost*. Check the lesson plans for additional ideas.)

Science: Animal Classification

Also, if you are continuing the animal classification game begun in the lessons of *Blueberries for Sal*, add gull, starfish, crab, fish, etc.

Naming Pets

It is fun to name pets. Sometimes pets are named for characteristics; sometimes for color, etc. How does Jenny decide on the names for her kittens? (Pumpkin is named for his color, and Smoky is also named for his color.) Does your family have pets? How did you choose their names? Remember how Sarah names Buttercup's babies in *The Little Rabbit*? There are seven baby bunnies and Sarah names them for the days of the week!

Making Decisions

Jenny raises two kittens during her summer vacation. But, when the time comes for her to return home at summer's end she can take only one of them home with her. What is her problem? (She loves them both.) How does she arrive at her decision? (After accepting the fact that she can only take one kitten home, Jenny makes her decision based on the personality of the two pets. She decides to take the calm kitten home to her apartment, and leave the roving kitten with her Granny at the beach.) Do you think she makes a good decision?

Observation

How can you tell it is summer in the pictures of this story? Give hints: What kind of clothes is Jenny wearing? When do people enjoy swimming? When do birds build nests (picture opposite first page of story)? When do trees have lots of green leaves? When are there often big puffy white clouds and quick thunderstorms? If you and your child are extra observant, you will recognize that at the beach, even in the summer, it is sometimes cool. Look at the kittens lapping milk by the fireplace, and the warm socks that Jenny is wearing. In another picture Jenny has on pants and a hooded sweatshirt.

Part Two

Parent's Treasury of Creative Ideas for Learning Readiness

Parent's Treasury of Creative Ideas for Learning Readiness

The many ideas that follow may seem overwhelming at first glance. But take time, find a quiet spot and enjoy musing over the many possibilities. This list is not a *must do* list. Rather, it is composed of many suggestions. These activity ideas are to encourage and guide you as you create enjoyable times for your child, and to inspire your *own* creative ideas. They are certainly not meant to be done all at once! During these early childhood years, you will enjoy incorporating many of these creative ideas into the time you spend with your child.

Most suggestions include an explanation of how they help build a foundation of readiness in some area of your child's life. His readiness for relationships and academics comes in part from encouraging his curiosity and imagination, and from his sense of security born of memorable times spent with you. The suggestions are divided into categories so that you will be able to review them quickly and find what you need. Many of the suggestions will overlap the categories and you will see them more than once.

Now is the only early childhood you will ever be able to share with your child. These are golden years. It might be worthwhile to once again thoughtfully consider how you really want to spend your time. What could you put off until later in order to maximize and preserve these few precious years with your child? Perhaps that new project, full-time career, new car, new house or dream vacation can be put off for another year or two. Your sacrifice today will mean a stronger academic *and* emotional future for your child tomorrow. Your love, time and attention mean so much. In a child's world, there is simply no substitute for *you*!

Activities for Reading Readiness

Being Together
Talking and Listening

One of the major ways your child learns language is by listening to you. Talk with him often from the moment he is born. Just keep up a simple banter about what you are doing and how much you enjoy being with him. Tell him how much you enjoy dressing him, "Mommy loves to help you get dressed. Here goes the shirt. Now I'm putting on your shoes." Whatever you find interesting, just talk! Good speech patterns are an important part of reading readiness.

When your child actually begins to talk (beyond those first words we hold so dear), *listen* to what he says. It is amazing how easy it is to tune out our children. Make an effort to stop for a moment, listen and comment before returning to your task. It is the same simple respect you want for yourself. Each time you pause and actually *listen* to your child, he grows in self-respect and *you* receive the added benefit of really knowing *who* your child is.

Reading to Your Child

Having a parent read aloud is one of the sublime joys of childhood. Read to him often. And let him see *you* reading books for yourself. Children place value on what they see their parents doing. Isn't it amazing that your love of reading is part of the beginning of your child's reading readiness?

Read him a wide variety of things from very simple to more difficult read-aloud books. Include a simple comic strip now and then. (Comics are great for learning the important concept of *sequencing*.) Even when you read familiar stories, pause now and then and ask your child simple questions such as, "What happens next?"

Wordless Books

Another good way to learn sequencing is to use *wordless* books from time to time. Nancy Tafuri has a wonderful title called *Follow Me*, 1990, Greenwillow Publishers, ISBN 0688087736. This is a story told completely in pictures. From the illustrations of the front inside covers to the back cover a story unfolds of a young sea lion looking for friends. The pictures are warm and expressive. You can look at the illustrations first and then go back to the beginning, asking your child, "What do you think is happening? What happens next." Another popular wordless book is, *A Boy, A Dog, and A Frog*, by Mercer Mayer, 1992, Dial Books for Young Readers, ISBN 0140546111. In fact, there are actually four of these stories and you can buy them one at a time or in a set.

Rebus Stories

Children also love rebus stories. Rebus stories have recurring pictures in place of certain words within the story. A non-reader can follow along on the page and say the word for each picture as you pause during the narration. This simple activity teaches the important sight reading technique of following left-to-right on a page. Your child has to follow along to know the next picture. Check your library or bookstore for a book of rebus stories called *Picture Stories for Children*, by Irmengarde Ebrle, 1949 Delacorte Press, ISBN 0385293402. Also look for *P. B. Bear's Birthday Party* by Lee Davis, DK Publishing.

Give it Everything You've Got

Add both fun and meaning to all your reading by speaking dramatically, making appropriate noises for the story, and adding lots of actions, voices, and expressions. Have fun and laugh a lot! What your children get *out* of a story is often directly proportional to how much you put *in* to reading the story.

Your Child's Favorite Voice

There are times when a parent simply cannot fulfill his child's request to "read me another story, please!" For these times, there are now many good stories on cassette tape. But, an even more special solution to this problem is to make *your own* cassette tape of your child's favorite stories. *Your* voice and all your child's favorite sound effects are far more wonderful to your little one's ear than any professionally produced tape money can buy. These homemade tapes are a great gift surprise and wonderful for your child to enjoy when you might have to be away. An older sibling who enjoys reading and has drama "production capabilities" might enjoy making such a story tape and finding just the right background music and even props for sound effects!

Nursery Rhymes

Read nursery rhymes. This allows your child to hear "what his language can do" in the way of *sound*. Many childhood rhymes set the stage and make learning academics so much easier. Remember the rhyme "One, two buckle my shoe"? This is just one of many common rhymes that teach children the names of the numbers before they even know what numbers are. One day, when we decide to teach counting or teach them to recognize number symbols, the *names* of the numbers are already familiar to them.. "Oh, that's what two looks like!" might be your child's comment. An easy to find book is Maud and Miska Petersham's Caldecott award winning, *The Rooster Crows, A Book of American Rhymes and Jingles*, 1945, Macmillan Publishing, ISBN 0027731006.

Poetry

Read poetry together. Quote poetry and rhymes to your child often. There is so much language development that takes place from hearing poetry. Poetry helps a child learn the sounds his language makes. He begins to be aware of cadence and rhythms. He is enchanted by the word play of rhymes and ideas. He grows in the ideas of poetic awareness that will enhance even his prose writings in the years to come.

With poetry there is so much to recommend. Of course there are all the simple childhood verses and nursery rhymes. There are the amazing books from Dr. Seuss. Try the well loved poems from A. A. Milne in the books *When We Were Very Young* and *Now We Are Six*. An excellent volume of children's poetry edited by Helen Ferris is called *Favorite Poems Old and New*. For your young children, don't forget Robert Louis Stevenson. Stevenson's *A Child's Garden of Verses* is a great book to own. It comes from different publishers with different types of illustrations. Choose a version with the pictures you like the best. The *A Child's Garden of Verses* Dover Coloring Book, ISBN 0486234819, has large line illustrations that an older child could color with bright colored pencils and present as a gift to a very young sibling. Then read Stevenson's poetry together and enjoy!

A Right Word in Season

Also, use the various poems at applicable times. For instance, one Stevenson poem is about "wake up you sleepy-head." It is easy to remember, and you could recite it on mornings when you have to wake your child. There is a short poem about being at the seashore. Another of Stevenson's poems is about what he did one day while he was "sick and lay a-bed." Bring this wonderful poem

out and share it when your child is ill. There is a Stevenson poem about windy nights, and another about going to bed in summer while it is still light. Say, "I remember a poem about....." Your child will think it amazing that you sometimes have an appropriate poem for just the occasion! Years later, when he is sick, or there is a particularly windy night, he will remember your poems and the closeness you shared. He'll be grateful that you took the time to create those special moments.

Hand Games

Hand games and hand plays incorporate many activities at the same time. Often they are set to song or rhyme. Each of them holds a special delight for children. There are the very early childhood games of Pat-a-Cake and Peek-a-Boo, etc., and later Peas Porridge Hot, Peas Porridge Cold. There are the finger plays of early childhood like "Here is the church and here is the steeple, Open the doors and see all the people!" Or, "Two little blackbirds sitting on a hill, One named Jack and one named Jill. Fly away Jack. Fly away Jill. Come back Jack. Come back Jill." Remember the song "Little Cabin in the Woods"? A wonderful resource for such hand games and finger plays is the tape *Wee Sing: Children's Songs and Finger Plays*. This tape comes with a book that has the music, chords, lyrics and hand gestures. ISBN 0843137932. The tape can be found in local bookstores in the children's section and is a truly *great* resource for learning a new verse or finger play (or two) a week. You don't have to listen to all of it, or try to learn all of it at once!

As your child graduates from just watching *you* do the hand plays to imitating them *himself*, he is learning small motor control. You will both have fun reading the story *We're Going On A Bear Hunt* and doing the appropriate stamping and clapping motions. See other activities for *We're Going On A Bear Hunt* on page 91 of *Before Five in a Row*.

Singing

Singing together opens many avenues in which to share the details of life. This is because we tend to sing about what we are reminded of, what we are noticing, how we feel at the moment, etc. The verses of songs teach us about many different kinds of people and often the history of how they lived. Singing, also has traditionally been an activity that draws people together in times of happiness, celebration, sadness and grief. In addition, singing teaches the "language of music" to a child, the way talking to them teaches them to speak. Music can soothe emotions, melt away fears, or provide an outlet for wild exuberance and happiness. It can also release the depths of grief.

Music and Feelings

Indeed, singing can be a vehicle for expressing emotions. If it is a day of grief (like the day a pet dies or a special friend moves away) you might sing a made-up *sad* song for a while to define and validate these feelings. "I'm so sad 'cause Harry moved away...." The uniquely American musical style known as "the blues" came about for this

very reason. After a while the happier songs and melodies will follow once more. The famous hymn "It Is Well With My Soul" was written in the aftermath of just such a grieving process.

Music

Music is wonderful. It is also important to our lives. So, sing together. Sing often. Make a habit to look for books with children's songs, folk songs, patriotic songs, hymns, etc., and make music together! Your children will remember!

One resource for these kinds of songs is the *Wee Sing Tape Series*. These tapes have a large variety of wonderful childhood songs. They also come with a book of the music, chords and lyrics. You can quickly learn the words and tunes to many songs through this resource. Below are listed some of the titles in the *Wee Sing* series of cassette tapes:

Wee Sing Nursery Rhymes and Lullabies
ISBN 0843137940

Wee Sing Children's Songs and Finger Plays
ISBN 0843137932

Wee Sing—Sing Alongs
ISBN 0843138041

Wee Sing Fun and Folk
ISBN 0843138025

Wee Sing America—Patriots and Pioneers
ISBN 0843137991

Every six months or so, purchase a new *Wee Sing* tape and learn additional songs. If the amount of songs on each tape seems overwhelming, just learn a song or two. When your family has learned the songs, you can enjoy them together wherever you are. Ask for a tape for birthday or holiday gifts. The *Wee Sing* tapes are a rich resource of lyric material that will benefit your entire family for years to come.

*Hands to clap
Fingers that snap
Arms that sway
and Feet to stamp.
Toes to keep up
a single beat.
Music is fun!
Music is neat!*

Making Music

Along with singing and dancing, making and playing instruments is a childhood must! Many of us remember wearing a paper hat and happily banging on a pan with a spoon while loudly singing *Yankee Doodle*. You don't have to go out right away and purchase musical instruments. From the simplest household instruments like pots and pans, to beautiful homemade instruments, making music together is fun.

Additional Books

Go In and Out the Window, 1987 Metropolitan Museum of Art, ISBN 0870995006, (also available from Henry Holt and Co., ISBN 0805006281) includes many children's songs, with music and chords. As a special bonus, each song is illustrated by famous works of art from the Metropolitan Museum of Art. You can spend many enjoyable hours with this great book.

There is also a companion book called *Songs of the Wild West*, commentary by Alan Axelrod, Metropolitan Museum of Art, 1991, ISBN 0870996118 (also available from Simon & Schuster, ISBN 0671747754).

Dancing

Dancing is another outlet for creative energy, emotions and exercise. Make up dances together. Add in small tap dance steps like the shuffle-step-ball change, marching steps, or the box step of the waltz. If you are interested in more than just made-up dancing, get a video from your library and learn a few real ballet, jazz or ballroom dance steps. Add these in from time to time as you play together. But, don't *require* that your child "get it". Large motor control progresses differently in children at different ages. No two are alike. These kinds of activities will help your child grow in muscle control and coordination over a period of time. Keep it fun. Let your child's desire to imitate you guide him. At this age, there isn't a right or wrong way for your child to express himself through music. Let him sway to the beat, wave his arms, march or whatever he seems to enjoy. Don't forget to join in and have fun dancing with him!

Marching

Search your library for tapes or CD's of march music. Children's sections of bookstores have these tapes also. Create your own marching band and play whenever you can. Because most young children do not yet play melodies, playing rhythm instruments (drums, cymbals, triangle, wood block, rhythm sticks, etc.) to any kind of music they enjoy is lots of fun. Whether the melody comes from a family member playing an instrument or from cassette tapes, records or a CD player, your child will learn to *hear* the beat and begin to make his own music to accompany the melody. Let him make his own discoveries and try to keep such times of music fun and not a drill. (For young children interested in exploring melodies, traditional childhood instruments for creating melody include: xylophone, 8-note octave bell set, glasses or bottles with varying amounts of water to create an 8-note octave set and simple child-sized piano keyboards with color-coded notes.)

Children can make music by humming, yodeling, clapping, snapping their fingers and stamping their feet. Listen to the rhythms of the music and play your instruments or clap along to the beat. You can also clap certain beats and rhythms and have your child follow by imitating. This provides a wonderful beginning to the exciting world of music. Many adults never developed a love for music because they were never exposed to the joys of music in early childhood. Children are full of creativity and energy. Enjoy your child's abandonment in music and encourage him in every way you can!

Making Musical Instruments

There are many ways to make beautiful, long lasting musical instruments. Check out some books from your library by looking up: "Musical instruments—Construction—Juvenile," in the card file. Woodworking fathers and older siblings can team up to cut and sand six-inch blocks from two-by-fours. Glue sandpaper on one wide side of two blocks. Then they can be rubbed back and forth for a great rhythm sound. The plain side of the blocks can be clapped together for a different sound. Heirloom drums are made from chamois and leather cord. The chamois is wet when stretched over the top and bottom of a metal can or wooden form. Using wet leather cord, the top and bottom chamois are laced together over the drum form through holes punched in the skins. Then the chamois dries taught and makes a drum that will last a lifetime. Also, you can make maracas from gourds, or by using papier-mache and beans, etc. There are many more ideas for instruments, so keep looking for books at your library or bookstores.

Drama

Drama includes a wide variety of activities. First, there is playing *pretend*. Playing pretend is especially wonderful if you have a big box of *costume* clothes. These clothes can be cast off clothing of your own, or specially discovered items at thrift shops, etc. Often the most absurd or gaudy items in a thrift store make the most wonderful costumes! Even boys like to dress up in buckskins with a Davy Crockett hat. Or think of all the kinds of hats a boy might like: a cowboy hat, fireman's hat, policeman's hat, construction worker's hard hat, a miner's hat, army or football helmets, etc. Many children enjoy a cape from a super hero or a suit like their father's. Girls are naturals at this enjoyable pastime. From dressing up like "mommy" to brides, princesses and cheerleaders, little girls never tire of wearing costumes.

Storing Your Costumes

You can use an old or new trunk to store the costumes. Another good storage idea is a wardrobe box from a moving company. These boxes have a place to hang items on hangers and have additional storage room at the bottom for boxes of hats, shoes, etc. To make wardrobe boxes accessible for your child you will need to cut down the right front edge of the storage box and across the bottom front edge to make a "door" that swings open. Make a fastener to shut the wardrobe when play time is over.

If you have no place else to store your "costume department," even an empty drawer will do. Try to place a long mirror in a nearby location. Full-length mirrors are available at discount stores for about ten dollars and are often found at garage sales for less. And be sure to take a picture now and then for your own memories. Your child will enjoy looking back in twenty years and remembering the fun times he had wearing costumes.

Make Believe

Pretend can also mean pretending to be an explorer, a pilot, a spaceman, a ballerina, etc., (not to mention a lion or a tiger) with or without costumes and props! Imagination is what inspires writers, poets, playwrights, and artists. A good imagination is also useful for developing problem-solving skills. Read *Little Bear* by Else Homelund Minarik, 1957, Harper and Row, Publishers, ISBN 0064400044. Little Bear did a lot of pretending!

All Grown Up

Pretend also includes portraying real-life scenarios such as playing teacher, secretary, fireman, storekeeper, and having tea parties, playing house, etc. There are ideas about playing house and playing store in the section below under: Toys.

Putting on a Play

Besides just playing "pretend," your child may learn to stage small plays, especially if he has other siblings that are interested and will help with the parts. Costumes are great for these type of dramatic adventures.

Puppets and Puppet Shows

Drama also includes the use of *puppets* and *puppet shows*. You may begin by making or buying some puppets and putting on some simple shows. Soon, your child may want to stage some shows of his own. Encourage him and spend time watching his performances. At the same time, continue to create for him more sophisticated puppet shows using your own made-up stories or fairy tales and other childhood legends. You can also make up perfectly good puppet shows that simply showcase the real life events of a family, helping each other, working and playing together. Young children especially like to watch the events of a fictional child's life.

"All the World's a Stage..."

If you are into woodworking, build your child a puppet theatre out of wood. Or make one out of a cast off refrigerator box. (Check appliance stores that deliver. They could probably save you one.) Or just throw a full length table cloth over a table and sit in a low chair or on the floor.

When you put on a puppet performance for your child, include lots of dramatic voices and actions. Build suspense. Use humor. A puppet production from you is far better than just another television show or video. You are *real* life, and with you is real interaction. Your child will slowly gain a wealth of dramatic knowledge through these live, interpersonal experiences.

Videotaping it for Later

As he grows, if your child enjoys drama, he may want to do puppet shows for younger children or graduate to putting on his own plays. Some families might want to videotape favorite puppet shows or play productions. These home "movies" could be of the parent's production or the shows staged by the children themselves. Or they could represent a combination of both. These videos are a wonderful way to preserve precious memories. You may also want to create a special videotape of some of your child's favorite puppet shows and leave it as a surprise for your child to view when you have to be away.

A Trip to the Theatre

As your child grows in his knowledge and appreciation of drama, see if you can find quality children's performances at your local children's theatre, museum, or library, etc. Usually these will be advertised with a suggested audience age. Some children will be more interested in this form of entertainment than others. Live theatre provides artistic flights of pure joy and delight to little ones in this age group.

Coordination

Large Motor (Muscle) Control

Tumbling and Wrestling

Small children love tumbling and wrestling as long as it's not too rough. Their muscles become strong as they keep active, and traditionally this is a much-loved activity because it is time spent with a parent. Usually, the tired tumblers and wrestlers collapse in a heap with a close hug. What could be better?

Rolling Like a Log

Encourage your child to try rolling over something like a pillow. Let your child roll over you! The more time spent in play-exercise, the stronger your child will become.

Crab Walk

Remember? This is sitting on the ground and placing your hands down behind you on the floor. Now raise yourself up and "walk" using your feet and hands. Walk frontwards and backwards. Can you do it sideways? One day, after play-exercising, take your child to a pet store, aquarium, or fish market and let him see a real crab and how it walks!

More Ideas

For more ideas, search for good books of children's exercise at your library or bookstore. One excellent book is *Basic Movement Activities*, Book #1 in the Perceptual Motor Development Series, by Jack J. Capon, David S. Lake Publisher, ISBN 0822453002. If your library or bookstore doesn't have this book, perhaps they can order it for you. Other books in this series include *Ball, Rope and Hoop Activities*; *Balance Activities*; and *Bean Bag, Rhythm Stick Activities*. These books were created for primary grades so be careful to use wisdom in selecting movements for your young child. These books contain many types of activities that your young child *can* do and you will be able to use this book and the others in this series for years to come. Keep looking for good physical activity books, and mix old-fashioned books with modern ones for variety.

Balancing

You can begin *balancing* exercises by placing a bright-colored tape on the floor or carpet and "walking the line" along with your child. You can progress to a five- or six-foot two-by-four placed on the ground. Eventually, the board can be raised a few inches. (Be sure to use wisdom and keep safety first and foremost in mind in this exercise.)

You can also play balancing games like walking with a book on your head. Begin by walking slowly and then try walking faster. Have your child try walking while holding a giant armful of stuffed animals or holding a basket filled with stuffed animals. He may have to work to keep any animals from falling to the floor. The animals will also block his view so he cannot see where he is placing his feet. Perhaps your child would like to see if he can carry a tray with plastic water-filled cups. Is he able to do it without spilling? Can he walk while balancing a balloon on his head? (Obviously the key to success is walking so slowly that the balloon doesn't "blow" off as your child walks!)

There are many types of activities that continue to build balancing skills such as the old game of hopscotch and standing on one foot in games such as Simon Says. Riding scooters, big wheels, or tricycles help improve balance. In later years, most sports including roller skating, roller blading and ice skating require even greater balancing skills.

Hopping, Skipping, Galloping

The practice and mastery of these three movements also increases coordination. Make up games that make use of these movements and include them in some of your child's playtime. Also, traditional games such as Mother May I?, Simon Says, Follow the Leader, and Fox and Geese are all useful in developing coordination. Of these movements, skipping is probably the most difficult because it requires changing feet. We tend to use a dominant side. You might even see a pre-school aged child going up the stairs leading continually with his right foot or continually with his left foot, rather than in opposition. When going up and down stairs you can cheerful-

ly say, "*right* foot, *left* foot, *right* foot, *left* foot." By hearing you, and watching what you do, your child will imitate and eventually learn to alternate feet. He'll do this even if he does not yet fully understand the meaning of right and left. (Full understanding of right and left is considered a five- or six-year-old skill.) So, because skipping calls for alternating feet in a rhythmical way, it may be the last of these movements your child will learn. These movements will not be accomplished on the first try. Be patient and enjoy watching your child's progress during these early years. All three of these activities also help develop the large muscle groups, increasing large motor control.

Pushing, Pulling, Dragging

Pushing, pulling and dragging require that your child have a concept of the space around him. If, for example, he is pushing something and it bumps into something else, he will try again to place the object where he wants it. His muscle control and his ability to understand spatial concepts will improve as he has chances to try and test these movements, so provide many opportunities for him. Cardboard boxes of different sizes and weight are good for pushing. Small cars and other vehicle-type toys are also good for pushing. Do you remember moving a toy bulldozer around in the sandbox when you were young? Pushing, pulling and dragging are important dexterity and spatial concepts that *precede* reading, printing with a pencil, etc. Provide toys, space and lots of time for this sort of play.

Wagons or boxes with an attached rope, as well as specially designed pull-toys, are all good for pulling. (We don't see as many pull-toys today. Yet, they were a valuable means to learn pulling skills and spatial awareness. If you are talented in wood working, maybe you would like to make a special pull-toy—anything from a duck to a train, or that special heirloom wagon—for your child.

Playing Ball

Rolling a Ball

Sit on the floor opposite your very young child and face him. Sit with your legs in a V shape with your own feet close to or touching your child's feet. Roll the ball back and forth so that your legs channel the ball to the child's hands. (Before you get up, reach out and hold your child's hands and gently pull/rock back and forth. You can sing "Row, Row, Row Your Boat" while you do this exercise.) Your child can also roll the ball toward a specific target. Remember plastic bowling pins? You can set up cardboard tubes from paper towels or bathroom tissue. Let your child try to hit a group of these "pins" at first. Later, as his coordination improves, he can try to hit just one. You can also set up some of the tubes in different areas of a room to further expand your child's spatial awareness. You can make up many variations to this play. Large soft foam-type balls are good for this—they roll well but they won't hurt furnishings.

Catching a Ball

Playing catch is always fun. Use different sized balls, beginning with larger, soft or squishy rubber balls to make catching easier. As your child gains coordination and skill you can toss smaller and harder balls. It's also fun to use the new, large, plastic balls readily available in discount stores for a change of pace.

Throwing a Ball

Throwing a ball to a specific target takes more coordination and large motor control. Enjoy watching your child progress in this skill by allowing him time and providing a place to throw a ball. Much of his playtime will be on his own. You can help provide interesting variations to his play. For instance, take a box and cut a large hole in the top or on one side. Draw a line for your child to stand behind (make it easy at first, really close) and let him try to throw the ball through the hole.

Lay a hoop on the ground and see if he can toss the ball into the hoop. (It counts even if the ball bounces out.) Set baskets in different corners of the room and see if your child can hit the baskets. He could also try to *bounce* the ball once and have it drop into the basket. (A very young child can *carry* the ball to the different baskets and drop it in. Be sure to praise his work.) Making up many variations keeps this skill-increasing activity mere play. (Any of these ideas can also be done with a bean bag at first, and later with a ball.)

You can also pantomime or *pretend* throwing. In your pantomime of throwing, use good form and be sure to act out the results! Jump up and down when you've "hit" your target, etc. If you don't "hit" your target put on a sad face. Or if your *child* has hit the imaginary target jump up and down, pat him on the back and shake his hand in congratulations. There are many ideas for this type of play under catching, bouncing, etc.

Bouncing a Ball

Drop the ball and catch it again. This is a more difficult step. Have fun practicing together. Then you take the ball and bounce it one time to your child and he bounces it one time back. When you can do this well, continue with more bounces in between.

Dribbling a Ball

Learning to "dribble" a ball is an advanced skill. There are lots of junior high students who have not mastered dribbling. Demonstrate this skill from time to time and watch as your child tries it himself. Remember—don't laugh at the predictably funny early results. Time and encouragement will help him master this complex skill!

Playing with Balloons

The subject of small children playing with balloons naturally brings up the possibility of children choking on them. You can still enjoy these old-fashioned childhood toys as long as you provide proper supervision. Get a large balloon. Blow it up and play catch with it. Balloons are not as predictable as balls and therefore require more control to both throw and catch them. Their very unpredictability is what makes them so much fun.

Blow up several balloons and try tossing them up one by one while your child tries to keep them all off the floor by constantly batting them back up. This requires a great deal of scurrying around. (Toss two up and play for a while. Now try three, etc.) Find two small brooms and play indoor "hockey." You will be able to think of other games using balloons. The time you spend playing and having fun with your child has the added benefit of increasing his large motor control. **Note:** Just remember to put the balloons away in a child-proof place after using them.

Blowing Bubbles

Blow bubbles and let your young child try to catch them. This can be fun out in the yard or at bath time! Or, let your child try to "steer" bubbles through a hoop of some kind by blowing on them, etc. If you are outside, it will be an extra attraction to see the beautiful colors on the surface of the bubbles!

An excellent resource is the book *Bubbles* from the Boston Children's Museum. It is written by Bernie Zubrowski, 1979, Little Brown Publishers, ISBN 0316988812. One of the wonders of this book is making *giant* bubbles outdoors. If you make these giant bubbles, don't forget to make some at night. As they drift skyward, shine a flashlight on them. It is truly an *amazing* sight!

Development of Small Motor (Muscle) Control

The development of small motor (fine muscle) control is basic to handling a pencil for writing, holding a needle for sewing, using hands to comb hair and tie shoes, picking up items and placing them where you wish, etc. As with other types of physical development, fine motor control comes at different times for different children and is not related directly to intelligence. All the activities and play of early childhood help facilitate this development.

Playing "Patty Cake" or "Peas Porridge Hot" with your young child helps him learn hand-eye coordination and develops fine motor control. So does setting dominoes on edge as well as hitting a toy work bench with a wooden hammer. Almost all physical play helps develop fine motor control. The time spent in this type of play is so important!

Playing With Puzzles

Playing with puzzles is especially good for fine motor development. To complete a puzzle your child has to pick up pieces and place them in a specific spot. Beginner's puzzles have fewer, but larger pieces. By completing these beginner's puzzles your child will build his confidence and move on to puzzles with smaller and more numerous pieces. (There is another excellent aspect of puzzle play. Your child is learning to see a shape and find a corresponding hole where it will fit. Learning to match shapes will help him later in letter recognition.)

Compartmental Organization

Compartmental Organization is another activity that helps young children develop small muscle control. (Small muscle control really means "small movements" like writing, or buttoning a shirt as compared to throwing or running.) To make the compartments, use a muffin pan (or mini-muffin pan) or an egg carton. (If you use egg cartons, select a twelve or eighteen-egg Styrofoam carton and be sure to wash it with soap and hot water.) Now, find some items to sort into the compartment spaces. (Watch the size of these items, depending on the age of your child. Be sure to keep close supervision over this activity to prevent accidental swallowing.) You could use small shells, pebbles, beans, etc. You can use a pile of coins and your child can put one of each denomination in each compartment. So each compartment would then have a penny, a nickel, a dime, etc. He doesn't have to know what these coins are called, he can just sort them by color and size.

Sorting Games

There are many games you could invent using these types of containers and small sorting items. Another yummier variation is to reduce the number of container spaces by cutting the egg carton in half. Then you can use M&M candies and have your child sort them by color. Or, you can use the muffin tin and let your child put one of each color in each muffin space. Continue to think up simple new ideas for compartmental organization and your child will be thinking as well as using his eyes and hands to accomplish his play-tasks.

Threading and Lacing

Make some batches of different colored large hole macaroni. (Color the pasta by using food-coloring while cooking. Then spread out the colored pasta and let it dry.) Provide shoelaces or thick string and let your child string the pasta. If he is very young, any way will do. If your child is older, he might want to try sequencing the colors so that a pattern develops. He could copy your pattern or make up one of his own. Maybe he could decorate a portion of his room with these garlands.

Take brightly colored poster board and cut figures from it. In the fall, use orange and cut out a seven- or eight-inch diameter pumpkin. Take a paper punch and punch holes every half inch around the perimeter of the pumpkin, about one-half inch in from the edge. Use a matching or contrasting corrugated paper ribbon (you know, the kind that curls) and let your child "lace up" the cardboard figure. Tie in a bow at the end. When he is finished, have him dictate to you an inscription for the pumpkin and send it to an aunt or grandparent. This same activity can be done with red poster board and big hearts for Valentine's Day, or simple fall leaves, four-leaf clovers, Christmas trees, or anything else corresponding to the seasons. Because he is making a card or gift, your child feels more productive and he is working on new shapes and colors at different times. The exercise of "lacing" is an important addition to the improvement of fine motor control. When you someday begin to teach letters and printing, your child's fine muscle control will be more suited to the task!

Bigger is Better

We'll talk more about art in the "art" section. Remember that for a young child, learning to hold a fat piece of chalk, washable marker or crayon and then getting it to do what he *wishes* is definitely a fine motor skill. These items are all made in "fat" sizes because they are easier for little fingers to hold and manipulate. If you will wait to use slim pencils until closer to school age, and keep the art items including paint brushes of the "large diameter" variety, your child will experience less frustration. (School teachers often say that they have to help many children re-learn to hold a pencil. How a child holds a pencil is important because as he spends longer and longer amounts of time writing, his hands and arms will tire quickly if he is not holding the pencil correctly. So if a child starts trying to grip a thin pencil at an early age when his coordination is immature, he may develop bad habits. Then at age five or six when he begins writing, it may be more dif-

ficult for him. This is another reason to wait on thin pencils and pens until later.)

Cutting and Pasting

Included in the world of art is cutting and pasting. These activities also require a certain amount of fine motor control and as time is spent pursuing these activities, fine motor control is improved. If your child is asking to try cutting, let him try. If he becomes frustrated and quits, just put the scissors away for another try at another time. (See special ideas for beginning cutting in the "Art" section.)

Pasting can be accomplished with old fashioned white paste. Or, try the newer glue sticks. Some of these sticks have a colored glue that lets your child *see* where he is gluing. The color fades away as the project dries.

Clay and Dough

Creative time with clay or soft modeling-dough is a wonderful way to get a child's ideas and fingers working together. Sometimes store bought dough-related "factories" fail to keep a child's imagination active beyond the initial week or two of play. But there is so much to activate your child's imagination and spark his creativity as he learns to roll out long ropes of clay which he can coil into useful or fanciful objects.

Learning to mold and sculpt animals and other items continues to increase his use of imagination and strengthens his fine motor skills. Begin making animals by rolling a ball shape or fat log shape and adding balls or rolls for head, legs, etc. Pinch up ears and roll some fine ropes for tail, mane, etc.

With some quick tips from you, your child will learn to interpret, with clay, both what he sees around him, and the things he imagines. Right at home you have so many household items that can make modeling a time of fun and creativity. We will talk about some of these ideas in the "Art" section, under Sculpture, pages 135-136.

Bath Time

From a parent's point of view, bath time can be a chore to be hurried through, or it can be anticipated as another special portion of the day spent together. We recommend finding ways to make this a delightful time, because time spent together is too important to waste!

Bubbles

At bath time, you can blow bubbles for your child to catch. He can blow some for you to catch. You can laugh a lot! At the same time your young child is having so much fun with you, he is also learning how to judge distance as he comes nearer and nearer to catching the bubbles.

Floating Toys

You can hold air-filled toys (like a rubber duck) under the water and let them pop up as a surprise. Your child will soon be holding toys under the water and watching them spring up. In his own experimenting he will find that some toys work better than others for this fun.

Washcloth Games

Try the washcloth game. Start with just a wet washcloth and call out various features of your child's face. "Wash your cheeks. Now wash your nose. Now wash your chin, ears, forehead, throat, neck, etc." Let him wash each feature as you call them out. Now soap up the wash cloth and call

out hands, feet, knees, legs, chest, etc. Does your child need help with his back? Soap up his back and draw his initial or a heart on it. Can he tell what you are drawing? (Someday this will be fun with guessing each letter or number.)

Pour it On

Bath time is a good opportunity for your child to engage in the wonderful world of pouring. Have various sizes of pitchers and other containers. Let him pour from one vessel to another. Divide the containers and pour into some of "his" while he pours into some of "yours." Or pretend to have a party using plastic cups and pitchers as teapots, tea cups, etc. Sometimes you will play with your child and be a participant. Other times you can just watch (or sit near and catch up on some reading) while he spends luxurious time playing and pouring.

Alphabet Bath

If your older child is becoming interested in letters, you can buy some of the plastic foam letters at children's toy stores. These stick to the wall over the bath tub. You can recite some of the wonderful children's alphabet stories as your child puts up each letter. Some of these stories are *A is for Annabel* by Tasha Tudor, 1954, Rand McNally, ISBN 0809810409, and *ABC Bunny* by Wanda Gag. *ABC Bunny* is in your list of story titles for *Before Five in a Row*. This would also be a great activity to do in the kitchen with the magnetic letters on the refrigerator or dishwasher, etc. You can read the story while your child places upper case letters and then read again for him to choose the lower case letters. If your child loves this activity, someday when he knows the letters, have him *alternate* upper and lower case as you read. There are many other wonderful alphabet stories to choose from, so be on the lookout for ones that strike your fancy.

Good Clean Fun

There are also soap-paints that your child can use to finger-paint on the wall of the tub. (Shaving cream might work here too, but don't let your child get it in his eyes.) He can make pictures or trace letters and then spend enjoyable time washing off the wall! He might pretend he's washing a car, or windows, or an elephant! Through all this play, arms, hands and fingers are working and growing more sure.

On another bath day, talk about the kinds of things you can find in the water. Things such as ducks, fish, boats, frogs, etc.

The delightful picture of Jesse Bear and his bath provides a wonderful reminder of just how fun bath time can be! Childhood is a wonderful time!!! (*Jesse Bear, What Will You Wear?* is one of the *Before Five in a Row* book titles.)

In the Kitchen

Pouring and Stirring

The kitchen is another place to practice pouring and stirring. Plastic containers, wooden spoons, pots and pans all can be used to make this favorite pastime great fun. When your child is older, he may want to experiment with plastic measuring cups, finding out how many cups fills a quart pitcher, etc.

Cutting Up in the Kitchen

The kitchen is a place to use cutting and chopping skills. Even a small child may want to help you cut up a banana, apple pieces, or other soft food with dull butter knife. Be sure to admire his work and encourage him in any way you can. The smile on your face will tell him a great deal. (If you play this favorite game, be sure to explain the difference between the butter knife and mother's sharp kitchen knives!)

Little Helpers

A young child can often hold a dustpan while you sweep, or he can perform other little duties that help him feel important and productive. Even if you later need to put some finishing touches on his work (and remember, there is a vast difference between the work of a three-year-old and a six-year-old), your encouragement *now* will make him feel loved and important. This will cause him to want to do an even more efficient job when he is older.

Bon Appetit

Make a recipe with your child now and then. Let's make a "circle" lunch. Start by making some gelatin jigglers (or wigglers). Maybe your child can pour two small packages of gelatin into a bowl. *You* pour in 1 1/4 cups of boiling water and stir till dissolved. Pour into an 8 x 8-inch pan and place in the refrigerator. Now, for that circle lunch! Let your child cut circles out of sandwich bread with a large biscuit cutter. You spread them with peanut butter and jelly or whatever you like. If your child is old enough, let him peel a carrot with a carrot peeler. Then you cut it cross ways into circles. Add some orange slices cut in circles. Then see if your gelatin jigglers are set. Using a small biscuit cutter and perhaps a donut hole cutter, let your child cut circles out of the gelatin. If he is very young just let him cut as he wishes. If he is older and his coordination more mature, suggest to him that cutting the circles very close together will result in more shapes with less waste. If you have a round plate and a round glass, he will be able to see more circles. Is your dining table round? Eat your lunch and sing a "round" like "Row, Row, Row Your Boat", or another song like "Ring Around the Rosy."

Getting in Shape

On another day make some gelatin jigglers. With cookie cutters, cut into stars, squares, crescents, circles, etc. Let your child name a shape and then feed it to you. Then you name a shape and feed it to him. Laugh a lot!! Then pretend to "be" the gelatin wigglers, and wiggle all over. Laugh some more!

Can We Talk?

The kitchen is also a good place to talk with your child about what you do there. If your child likes to sit and listen to you talk, then describe the process of making spaghetti. "First, I boil a pan of water...then I....", etc. Talk about crispy lettuce for the salad, or the crunchy carrots and let him enjoy a crunchy bite.

Kitchen Safety

The kitchen is full of colors, tastes, textures, and things to smell. Don't forget to go over basic safety tips about hot ranges, ovens, and sharp knives, etc. You can say, "When I cut the celery, I have to be very careful with the knife so I don't cut my finger." While you are cooking, your very young child will have fun playing on the floor with pans, spoons and other kitchen wonders. Don't forget the plastic bowls that nest together. Put on the lids. Now they stack!

Pots and Pans

Pots and pans have always been a source of pleasure and creative material for young children. They are fun to hold, fun to clang together, and can make a great hat—a la Johnny Appleseed! Old pans are the recipient of many an imaginary dirt-stew or leaf-soup which is usually stirred vigorously with a wooden spoon. Remember, a child-sized set of pans may hold some intrigue, but the pans in your kitchen are usually special because, of course, they are YOURS!

At the Store

Trips to the store with your young child along can be a trying experience. But, with a little preparation you can even maximize *this* time and turn it into a favorite outing.

So Much to See

The grocery store is full of interesting foods. There are bright colors, like oranges, eggplants, and a veritable rainbow of peppers. There are also different textures. Try handing your young child a coconut and watch the look on his face! The freezer aisle has things that are cold. Let him feel something from that compartment. Some stores even have live shell fish and other interesting items to see.

Organization

With your three- or four-year-old, discuss the fact that the manager of the store has organized things into certain aisles. That helps you shop more quickly. Talk about what is on the different aisles. Say, "Look! They have organized the frozen food in this aisle," or "Did you notice the canned vegetables are mostly on this aisle?" Show him the chicken and meat section. See if your child begins to remember where things are in your store from trip to trip. The concept of "organization" is important and discovering how the grocery store is "organized" is a fun, easy way to introduce this concept.

Talk it Over

Have fun calling out the names of vegetables when you are in that section. Read the cans, "carrots, beets, spinach, okra, black-eyed peas." Even with your younger child you can help him notice that some items come in bags, some in cans, while others are in packages or bottles. Hand him something from the frozen food aisle and watch his expression. It's sooo cold! Talk to your child about what you are doing. "I'm squeezing the bread gently to see if it is fresh," or "I'm looking for the reddest tomatoes. I don't really care for the green ones," etc.

Much of the poor behavior a child might exhibit in a store may have its roots in being ignored. So keeping up a chatter, "Doesn't this lettuce look fresh!" or "Have you ever seen such red strawberries?" is an easy way to turn this mundane task into a fun adventure in learning readiness.

On another trip to the grocery store talk with your four-year-old about farmers who grow the foods, dairy farmers and cattle ranchers, etc. When you get to the checkout counter you can discuss the fact that you pay money for the groceries. This money pays for the store and its employees as well as paying the farmers, etc., for their products.

Weights and Measures

On another shopping trip, briefly introduce the subject of scales to your child. Find a lemon and a grapefruit. Let your child hold them and ask him which is heavier. Explain that a scale measures the weight of an item. Now weigh the two fruits one at a time. Say, "You were right! The grapefruit *is* heavier. The scales say so, too." (You may see your child playing store and "weighing things" in the future!)

Shopping List Bingo

The following idea takes some serious preparation. If it sounds like fun to you—try it. Give your child a piece of cardboard or posterboard (8 1/2" by 11"). This card will contain six (to twenty) squares in which you have drawn the vegetables and other items you are expecting to purchase. (Or, you can cut pictures from the food sales page of your paper.) Then take your child to the store and give him a small sheet of colored dot stickers. As you shop for the items on your list, your child is supposed to watch closely. When he sees you put in your shopping basket an item that matches the card, he can place a sticker on that square. If he fills up his card by the time you are finished he wins a small prize. Obviously you would not do this for every shopping trip, but now and then it could make shopping a special memory for your child.

Grocery Store Scavenger Hunt

For your older child, give him a small picture list of a few items and accompany him as he searches them out. He then chooses the items and adds them to the cart. No throwing!! The eggs can break! Thank him for his help.

Some of these ideas might sound impossible when you are hurrying to complete your shopping. There will be times when you simply do not have the time. Yet, as adults we need to remember that we don't really have more important things to do than to love our children. So try to include at least a little "something interesting" in your time together. And lots of smiles are always good! Don't forget that at the store you can sing favorite songs together quietly as you travel the aisles. Waiting in line at the checkout stand is a great opportunity to do hand games, tell a story, or even catch up on some interesting news from your child.

Just For the Fun of It

And consider taking a "non-buying" trip to the store now and then. This would be more like a mini-field trip where you can concentrate on exploring the store together (maybe going where your *child* would like to go) looking, touching, and talking in an unhurried way. You might also do this when you only have an item or two that you need.

Mother's Helper

When you come home, your three- or four-year-old would probably love to help you put away the boxed and canned goods. Maybe you could arrange it so that your canned good section is on a low shelf that he could reach. You can show him how you like the shelf arranged and he will probably enjoy fixing it just the way that pleases you!

Toys

A quick review of toys: Toys are "whatever is around to play with." They can be familiar household or homemade items. And of course they can also be ready-made toys purchased or received as gifts from the store. Children have always allowed their imaginations to roam free as they find things to play with and then make up scenarios to go along with these items.

There are traditional toys such as blocks, wooden and metal cars, trucks, wagons, riding toys, dolls, stuffed animals, and many others. And, there are the newer toys of plastic, those that wind up, and new types of riding vehicles, etc. Of course, there are some card or board-type games which require more thinking skills than exercise but right now we're talking about the toys that a child plays with, manipulates and rides, etc.

What's a Good Toy?

Some of the things you might want to consider when you are making or purchasing a toy for your child are: Will he be able to make good use of his imagination? Do the toys demand the physical use of muscle groups to improve his coordination? Are they made of high quality materials to be long lasting?

Good toys will last through many stages of your child's life. For instance, a two-year-old will play with a good set of blocks and use just a few pieces

making a wobbly tower. As he grows, he will use more and more blocks. His imagination will progress into larger and more magnificent projects. You don't have to monitor when he is ready for the next stage. He will just grow naturally in his use of this versatile toy. One day you will just see his wobbly tower become a solid tower—perched atop a steady building! Playing with blocks increases fine motor coordination and allows limitless use of imagination. It is beneficial to choose quality toys which leave room for unmonitored advancement over many seasons of your child's growth.

In addition, you will also want toys that allow your child to utilize his muscles and help improve coordination. Whether it is the fine motor skills gained by playing with blocks, dominoes, etc., or large motor skills honed by playing ball, or pulling a wagon, good toys are an important part of childhood growth.

When Less is More

Toy stores today are filled with wonderful, creative toys such as ready-made doll houses that come complete with every detail included. (Playmobil® toys are unusually great for inspiring imaginative play.) As wonderful as this new generation of "supertoys" are, there may be some *additional* benefits to simpler, less-expensive toys. For instance, you might want to build a large wooden house with rooms and two or three floors. Let your child have a hand in painting the rooms and in making furniture from scrap items around your house. (You can also build a barn, stable, fire station, etc.) Match boxes, spools from thread, cardboard, blocks of wood, colored paper and pieces of material, etc., all make items that can be used in these structures. You will see growth in your child's creativity expressed in desiring an item, thinking of how it can be made, constructing it and then modifying it, and finally decorating the piece. This will be a far greater learning experience than using all store bought toys. As your child grows, he will replace his early handmade items with more sophisticated ones that he has made. And of course you can always buy the "supertoys" when your child is older. Also, quality-made, simplified dolls and teddy bears are perennial childhood favorites.

Heirloom Toys

Above all, the toys you choose should be durable and something of lasting value. Adults value things that last, from fine antiques to special relationships. Children can learn that special things have value, too. When your child is grown he will look with pleasure on the fine set of wooden blocks he played with as a child. Perhaps his children will continue the tradition of happy play with the very same blocks. So many of the toys purchased today at the store are poorly made from inexpensive materials. Some have so many moving parts that small hands soon break them. Fewer *good* toys are far better than quantities of poorly designed toys made from cheap materials.

So, for the most part, look for quality toys, made of pleasing, fine and durable materials. Toys that have very little mechanical parts, but leave room for vast amounts of imagination and muscle

power to "make them go" are often better than the latest "supertoy." These are the kinds of toys that stand a chance of becoming favorites of this generation and lasting into the next. (For a fascinating look at older classic toys, request this book from your library: *Toyland: Classic Illustrations of Children and Their Toys,* Ed. by Pamela Prince. Read the introduction and look at the beautiful pictures to find ideas for today!)

Quality toys, wisely chosen create a "busyness" in children that gives them a profound sense of self-sufficiency and contentment. These early attempts at "self-employment" can lead to a lifetime of successful work habits. And oh what fun they have in the process!

Blocks

Wooden Blocks

Blocks come in many sizes, colors, shapes and materials. There are the old-fashioned wooden square blocks that have bright letters, numbers, and sometimes even animals on them. There are wood blocks like you might find in a nursery school. These blocks are easy to make if you have woodworking equipment. Made out of two-by-fours, they can be cut into squares, rectangles (4, 6, 8 and 12-inch lengths), and triangles of various descriptions (right and scalene, etc.). Sometimes there are rounded arches cut out of the rectangles to make bridge-like pieces. In addition cylinder shapes are used for pillars, etc. (These homemade blocks must be carefully sanded smooth.) There is a beauty, mass and warmth in wood that even a small child begins to appreciate at an early age. Just lifting and using heavy wooden blocks helps build young muscles! Using large blocks on the floor requires your child to bend, sit and then get up for more, which continues the physical exercise hidden in this special play. In addition, large blocks build large forms (such as houses, boats, etc.) that a doll, or stuffed animal can be placed into, making your child's buildings both fun *and* useful. Today we also have large, plastic interlocking blocks and other "building toys." These can be an interesting addition to your collection of building blocks when your child is a bit older.

Imagine That!

Blocks also release the imagination. With blocks your young child progresses from the important stacking phase to eventually building complete cities and worlds. Isn't it amazing that his imagination will progress someday to be able to "see" entire cities, farms, castles, etc., in a scattering of plain old blocks! It seems like a miracle. You may build a house or barn with blocks and your young child will want to imitate that building. But, leave lots of time for him to play alone and develop his own ideas, too. When something he has been working on doesn't turn out the way he desires, rather than let him be so distressed he wants to "quit," try mentioning that perhaps a bulldozer might push away the rubble and leave room for that new project! These small creative "helps" from you at an opportune moment may reverse an unhappy mood, and set your child on an entire afternoon of satisfied play.

The Joy of Building

When your child has thought out an idea (no matter how simple), completed it by himself and is satisfied, something very special has happened. He has begun to enter into the joy of creation. The satisfaction involved in this type of play can have long lasting results. Beyond physical coordination, beyond imagination, building with blocks, even at a young age, can produce such a satisfying work that it may continue to release the productive, creative impulse well into adulthood.

A Lifetime Investment

Good sets of building blocks can play an important part in the mental, physical and emotional development of your child! If you don't have the ability to make a quality set of wooden building blocks at home, they are readily available for purchase, but require a substantial investment. If possible, visit a store which supplies nursery and pre-schools with furniture and toys. Find out the cost of block sets and consider them among your purchases. Or, perhaps you can let interested relatives know that these sets of blocks would make fine gifts for birthdays or Christmas, etc. The company called "Constructive Playthings" carries superb unit blocks. Call for a catalog 1-800-448-4115 and say you are a "Teacher". When you receive your catalog, find the section that is labeled Small Group Sets Unit Blocks and Large Group Sets Unit Blocks. There are many other types of block sets listed that could supplement later. A good set of blocks is a lifetime investment. Perhaps no other single toy can teach a child so many learning, readiness and creative thinking skills!

Sandbox

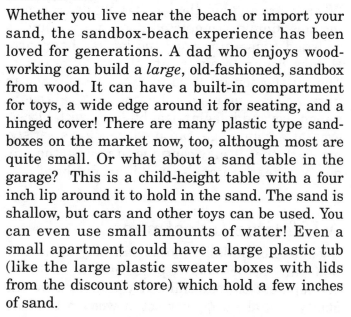

Whether you live near the beach or import your sand, the sandbox-beach experience has been loved for generations. A dad who enjoys woodworking can build a *large*, old-fashioned, sandbox from wood. It can have a built-in compartment for toys, a wide edge around it for seating, and a hinged cover! There are many plastic type sandboxes on the market now, too, although most are quite small. Or what about a sand table in the garage? This is a child-height table with a four inch lip around it to hold in the sand. The sand is shallow, but cars and other toys can be used. You can even use small amounts of water! Even a small apartment could have a large plastic tub (like the large plastic sweater boxes with lids from the discount store) which hold a few inches of sand.

Many types of home implements can be used in a sandbox—pot pie tins, small and large gelatin molds, and sieves. Large spoons, some sticks, rocks, plastic cups and pitchers with a little water are useful, too.

Pounding Box

You know, the type of little work stool that has pegs which your child pounds with a hammer? Then he turns the work bench over and pounds them back the other way. It takes hand-eye coordination to hit the peg and no small amount of persistence to hit it enough times to get the peg through. The trick for parents has always been to keep a close enough eye on their child that he doesn't tire of the game and begin to hit things that aren't his work bench! There are great benefits in this kind of work-play for your child however, which are important to his fine motor development.

Child-Sized Power

If you happen to have a construction site nearby, you might drive over and sit and watch some big machinery moving dirt, tearing up and removing old concrete, etc. Even small children may love the "big" exciting, powerful activity done by these kinds of machines. Interestingly, one of the best-selling children's videotapes in recent history is a simple, homemade tape which shows bulldozers, dumptrucks and roadgraders moving earth. Children seem to be fascinated by watching this type of activity for hours! Perhaps you could even create your own videotape of these gigantic earth-moving machines to watch over and over again. Then your child may re-create this type of real life action in hours of sandbox activity!

Pots and Pans

Pots and pans have always been a source of pleasure and creative material for young children. They are fun to hold, fun to clang together, and can make a great hat—a la Johnny Appleseed! Old pans are the recipient of many an imaginary dirt-stew or leaf-soup which is usually stirred vigorously with a wooden stick. You can search garage sales and thrift shops for interesting pans. But, your child may consider *your* cast-off pans a treasure because, of course, they are YOURS!

A Home of His Own

By the time your child is four years old he has probably begun to play house, mimicking the life he sees around him. You can help in these ventures by providing some basic "props" such as play stoves, sinks, etc., made of sturdy boxes and bright non-toxic paint. Find an old phone at a thrift store or flea market and let him pretend. Thrift stores and flea markets, as well as your own used, kitchen items, can yield child-sized items with which to play house. The more basic you make the furnishings, the more creative your child will be with them. Remember, he is the one who can "see" a city where there is only a pile of plain blocks.

An invaluable "ideas" resource for these types of play activities is a set of *Childcraft*. This set of fifteen volumes is packed with information, projects, and good old-fashioned common sense. Written in the 1930s, and continually revised, there is no substitute for the wholesome suggestions for play, singing, dance, art, exploring the world of science, etc.Note especially chapters titled "Making the Most of Your Home" in Volume 8, and "Nursery Years", Volume 13! Check your library for *Childcraft* and watch book sales, garage sales, and thrift shops. We recently found a beautiful 1961 set in like-new condition for $15.

Playing Store

Playing store is fun, too. A woman once said she played store at an old kitchen table which was designed to pull out to accommodate extra leaves.

She would pull the table apart and stand in the center, running items past her on one side of the table and ringing her "register" on the other side. There is no limit to the creative ideas that you and your child can express in this enjoyable pastime. Keep a box of empty cartons, cereal boxes, and cans (be sure they are not sharp) to use for playing store, and a white apron for the cashier! As your child grows older, playing store will offer an opportunity now and then to teach a number concept, so be ready to give insight at that special moment. This is especially good when it is your *child* who comes to you with a question that you can help with. (Enjoy that moment of growth when your child has his *own* idea to make dollar bills and use small items for pieces of money! Isn't childhood wonderful!!) Use discernment in when to "add" to your child's play. Remember that he is learning vast amounts of information by watching what goes on at a store and playing it out in his *own* manner at home.

Large Boxes

Boxes can be the ultimate toy. Like wooden blocks, they can be anything a child wants them to be. They come in all sizes and shapes. Huge refrigerator boxes (or other large appliance boxes) can be caves, houses, castles, or anything your child can imagine. A good source for these kinds of boxes is your large appliance dealer. When your child is three or four, try leaving a large box in the yard, garage, or your recreation room. Don't say anything other than, "You can have this for anything you'd like." See what he does! Remember, it may take a day or two for your child to think out a plan.

Note: Look for an amazing storybook called *Christina Katerina and the Box,* by Patricia Lee Gauch, Coward, McCann & Geoghegan, Inc., ISBN 0698206827. Christina may seem a bit demanding, but her imagination knows no bounds when it comes to making creative use of a box. This book is probably too old for your child now, but if *you* read it, your imagination will be sparked. Then you will be excited to provide boxes and opportunities for your child to launch himself into the creative world of box play!

Small Boxes

There are also cylindrical oatmeal, cornmeal, and salt boxes, and a great variety of other sizes of boxes. Collect some small empty boxes and hang them on the kitchen doorknob in a mesh bag (the kind that grapefruits or oranges come in). You can include tin canisters from tea or cocoa powder, and non-breakable, round spice cartons, etc. Let your young child create with these boxes while you cook.

Push Toys

When we speak of push toys we are thinking of any kind of toy that does not wind up and move under its own power, but requires a pushing action from your child. All (non-moving) toy cars, trucks, trains, boats, planes, construction and agriculture toys are included in this category. Regardless of the size of the toy, when your child pushes it and makes it do what *he* wants it to, he is learning hand-eye coordination, spatial awareness, using his imagination, and perfecting his fine and large motor skills.

Brains and Brawn

In the same way, a very young child pushing a chair, ottoman or heavy box is exercising and learning at the same time. This idea of the value of push toys seems so simple. There used to be so many. But now motorized and wind-up toys have replaced many of the more traditional ones. Why not begin your child's playtime with the traditional toys that take muscle power and imagination and leave the power toys for when he is older?

Pull Toys

Pull toys like wagons, boxes with a long rope attached, wooden toys on wheels with a string can have a place in the development of a child's coordination. For your child to play with these types of toys requires a certain understanding of the space that is around him. He has to maneuver the toy, while he isn't looking directly at it (usually) and keep it from bumping into the furnishings around him (usually). He thinks he is having fun with a toy that follows him around and he is! But, he is learning important things about the space around him at the same time. Kouvalis®, and Brio® make lasting quality pull toys and the toy store, FAO Schwarz, will have quality toys of all kinds including pull toys. For a free catalog, call Schwarz at 1-800-426-8697.

Dad and older siblings can brainstorm to make special pull toys for your younger child. These toys could become family heirlooms. Pull toys are becoming a thing of the past but with their absence we may also be passing up some important learning experiences. Better Homes and Gardens, *Wood, Favorite Toys,* ISBN 0-696-00037-7 is one good book on building toys.

A Ball for Every Occasion

There is a tremendous variety of different kinds of balls to play with. There are balls a foot and a half in diameter—great for tumbling over and trying to get small arms around. There are colored balls and clear balls, and balls for the bath tub.

Soft foam balls in all sizes and shapes and the new, squishy rubber balls with all the little rubber stickers have made ball play even more interesting. These are great for both indoor and outdoor play. Soft balls like these are also easier for tiny fingers to catch because they can grab, sinking their finger into the ball, and hold on. (Old fashioned bean bags, loosely filled, are also good for catching.)

There are balls to throw in a basket like a short basketball hoop or a bushel basket sitting on the ground. Footballs, tennis balls, even ping-pong balls can be used for a variety of play together. A four-year-old might like the game of two square. (Played like four-square but with only two boxes.) In this game you draw two connected boxes with chalk on a garage floor or driveway. The boxes should be four feet square. Then one person stands in each box and lift-hits the ball over the middle line. The other player lets the ball bounce once and then lift-hits it back over the line. You can move around inside and outside of the boxes, but the ball has to stay inside the boxes.

Surprise!

Young children love colors, shapes and *surprises*! Every now and then, find a new kind of ball and surprise your child with time to play. You could even take a tennis-ball-sized rubber ball and attach some bright colored streamers about three feet long. Make the streamers from colored parachute nylon (available at most cloth stores) or from crepe paper, ribbons, etc. Gather one end of each of the ribbons and tie them in a knot at the end. Cut a small slit in the ball and then use a screw driver to poke the knotted end deep into the ball. Test it to make sure it is exciting in flight, ribbons streaming out as it is thrown. Then, keep it for that special moment together. When the time is right, go outside and give it a throw. Watch your child's face! Have a great time.

Playing ball is something that children long to do and it is so easy. It can be done on the spur of the moment, and even fifteen or twenty minutes is appreciated by your child. There is no limit to all the different types of games and play you can enjoy with a ball, so have fun. The time spent together is indeed golden!

The Arts

There are three basic categories of art. Each category is made up of a different genre. In each genre there is an aspect of creating or performing the work itself. There is also another aspect in the appreciation of the works of others. Both of these areas are important to introduce to your child.

Visual Arts

(Generally known as Drawing, Painting, Photography, and Sculpture. Architecture might also be included here.)

Give Him a Hand

Art is splashy! Art is fun! Think of a giant, white poster board covered with your child's handprints in many colors and in a random pattern. Would he think making that was fun? Then let him stand on a stool or chair above his hand print painting. Let him take a paintbrush and drip some of the same colors over the hand prints so that random colored dots splash over the picture. Surely he would love that! Hang his creation in his room or on his door and he would be proud.

Art is everywhere. It is found in all of nature—colors, line, designs, form and textures. Man imitates and interprets what he sees and what he feels. The more you are able to stimulate your child's curiosity, the more he will have to express. You can encourage his curiosity by pointing out things that *you* find interesting and beautiful. Talk about the sunlight on the potted violet or the texture lines in the carpet. Art is indeed everywhere.

Gentle Guidance

Art is also quite personal. There aren't any right or wrong ways, just experimentation. (There may be more efficient ways to dip a brush into a color, or to clean it, but the creation—the work—is not right or wrong.) Therefore, be very careful not to demonstrate your ideas on his papers. For instance, if your child has drawn neat little leaves and you wish to show him a more artistic rendition, do it on a separate piece of paper. Then he can choose whether or not *he* wants to include *your* method in *his* work. Don't worry. Even if he does not use your idea right now, he will probably store the information to use later. Be careful how you criticize his work. Give him the same respect you would want and that you would give any other artist!

Your child's finished work comes from his emotions, his own personal stage of coordination, and from his imagination. Encourage him by providing time, materials and a place for him to try many different kinds of artistic endeavors. Your child will enjoy working with large-diameter washable markers, crayons and paint brushes. Tempera paint is a washable, opaque paint. Watercolors are fun too.

You might want to provide different sizes of paper. There are large tablets of paper and then smaller typewriter sized sheets. You also might want to have colored construction paper, colored tissue paper, and maybe some foil-type shiny paper on hand for special projects. Remember the different kinds of things you did with paper when you were young? You might have cut colored shapes and glued them to paper. You may have torn shapes and objects for that jagged look. Maybe you used a combination of construction paper pieces and pictures cut from magazines. Colored tissue-paper collages had a dimension you loved because the tissue crumbled as you glued it on. Your child is waiting for these experiences too!

Avoiding the Messies

"But it's messy!" you say. Well, yes. There is some mess to creating. Have your ever seen a professional artist's studio? By the time they reach that proficiency they need a room of their own in which to work! Yet, you know that these wonderful types of art activity are the delights of childhood. So, you'll want to be prepared. And a little preparation goes a long way. First, consider the best place in your home to do art projects. There needs to be light and some space. Then take steps to protect your furniture. Oil cloth is still available at fabric and discount stores and is great for covering tables used for art purposes. It can be wiped off easily, rolled up and put away. Also, you might want to protect your child's clothes. For a painting smock take an old, white dress shirt, (or one from the thrift store) cut the sleeves

to the right length for your child, and take off the collar. Put some velcro where the buttons and buttonholes are. Put the shirt on your child backwards and close up the velcro. Voila! an instant paint smock. You can decorate it with your child's name and with designs using puff paint if you wish. Have a hook ready where your child can place the smock when he has finished his creations.

The Cutting Edge

Scissors and paste or glue can be provided at the appropriate times. The blunt ended scissors are good for young children. Cutting practice begins with dark lines drawn on paper approximately six inches wide. (Wider pieces of paper frustrate young children as they try to cut long, straight lines.) Use *colored* paper, and your child's practice paper strips can be glued into connected circles to make a paper chain. The chain provides a great decoration for your child's bulletin-board or other area of his room. Remember that cutting curves is a more advanced skill and it will come later as his cutting skills grow. If your child prefers using his left hand, make sure the scissors are the correct ones for him.

Sculpture

Tools and materials for sculpting and modeling, like clay, modeling dough, and utensils are fun to use from time to time, too. We stated before that ready-made toys for use with soft modeling doughs are exciting at first. But, some of these toys may end up "on the shelf" because they do not stimulate creativity. Instead, try giving your child a variety of rolling devices like a child-sized rolling pin, or wooden dowels in different diameters and various lengths four to seven inches long. Add plastic forks, knives and spoons, as well as many plastic cookie cutters. (Watch garage sales and thrift stores for an infinite variety of inexpensive sculpting tools!) An old pizza cutter is fun, as well as an old garlic press (for your older child) to make fine hair-like strands for his projects (perhaps the mane of a horse!). Small gelatin-type molds create more fun. Dust them with cornstarch or flour before filling. Have on hand a small tin of unusual items that can be pressed into the dough as a decoration or just for texture. This is a wonderful place to use that old, junk piece of costume jewelry, old cracked buttons, or the throw-away items from your "kitchen" drawer—plastic bag tags, twisters, bent paper clips, etc. (Be careful to supervise the use of these kinds of materials with your very young child. But, with materials like these your older child can make such stunning decorations!) Also, see the Clay and Dough section on page 120.

Clay Vs. Dough

When you consider modeling clay versus the soft dough-type modeling substances, remember that clay is stiffer, more difficult to roll out. Rather than being detrimental, this stiff type of clay requires small hands to press and squeeze harder to achieve results. So, it is actually better exercise for little wrists and fingers! Perhaps you could use some modeling clay (comes in hardening and non-hardening varieties) and show your

child how to hand roll long ropes, which can be coiled into a plate or bowl shapes or made into pretzels, animals, etc. Demonstrate too, how to roll small, medium and large balls out of clay, some of which can be pressed into disks. These can be used for pretend food for tea parties, and doll houses, or food for stuffed animals! There are also types of play that are fun with the soft-type dough. So, have some of each on hand, play with different ones at different times to enjoy the variety.

There are many recipes for homemade soft-modeling dough. Here is a family favorite:

> 2 cups flour
> 3/4 cup salt
> 2 cups water
> 4 teaspoons cream of tarter
> 2 tablespoons cooking oil

Mix ingredients and stir together in a heavy saucepan, over medium heat, with a wooden spoon until it is no longer sticky and begins to form a ball. It is time to take the dough out of the pan and knead it. You can separate the batch into several balls and add different food coloring to each by kneading it in (wear rubber gloves). Or you can add one color per batch to the water before you mix the dough together. Take your dough out of the pan, cool a few minutes, then knead till smooth. Rubber dishwashing gloves can help insulate your hands from the warm dough while you knead. Store in plastic container or plastic bags in refrigerator, when not in use. Have fun!

In Laurie Carlson's book *Kids Create! Art and Craft Experiences For 3- to 9-Year-Olds*, there is a section about modeling with various homemade doughs. She gives five different recipes for modeling dough. The book has many other ideas, some of which you can use now and others later. It is a good book to request from your library. Then you can decide if it is a book you would like to own. *Kid's Create!* by Laurie Carlson, 1990, Williamson Publishing, ISBN 0913589519.

Stamp It

There is an almost infinite variety of art activities and techniques. Potato stamp printing has always been fun. Also, your child can make prints using a large, block rubber stamp. Having a whole fish for dinner? Make a fish print with *non-toxic* paint or diluted food coloring, lightly brushed over the surface. Press a large piece of paper against the fish. Now that you have the likeness of the fish, wash it thoroughly and fix it for dinner. What other items would be good for printing? Get an interesting texture by brushing some paint over a stiff piece of nubby fabric. Then use it like a stamp.

Finger Painting

There is also fingerpainting. Remember the thick paint and the slick paper? (Check teacher's stores and art supply stores for old-fashioned finger-painting paper!) Or you can paint with tempera or watercolors using a small sponge, a piece of sheep's wool, a feather or even a toothbrush (for spattering). There is no end to the interesting effects which you and your child can create. If you have a countertop or suitable table, let your very young child fingerpaint with chocolate pudding! Then you don't have to worry if some goes in his mouth! To make it more fun on a warm day, have the pudding cold! If you have a dark surface to work with, whipped cream is an interesting medium for four-year-olds. You can put some on a suitable counter or tabletop and he can use it like fingerpaint with the added ability to mound it up in a bas-relief manner.

Obviously, very young children will have to be carefully supervised and you will have to have easy projects for them to try. For instance, take a clean white paper plate. Let your young child take a large paintbrush (a craft brush or even the two-inch size like you paint woodwork with). Have him wet the brush and brush the water over the plate. Then take a smaller brush and let him wet his brush and dip into some water color. (If you take a small container to hold one color of paint, your child won't be tempted to put his brush in more than one color at once.) Let him drip some drops of the color he chooses on the wet paper plate. He can drip it or touch the brush to the plate. Let him see how the color spreads and how it runs. Then give him another color to try. Don't try to teach how the colors mix just yet. Let him do a lot of experimenting and noticing for himself. Later, your teaching will uphold *his* experience. Remember to do easy projects for the young artist. He will be less frustrated and he'll be happy to try again soon.

Bulletin Boards

In your child's room it would be great to have as large a bulletin board as you can manage. While he is very young, you might not want to use thumb tacks or push-pins. You can easily substitute teacher's putty (from teacher's stores or office supply stores) which holds paper without pins. Or you can use masking tape to put up pieces of your child's art work and also beautiful pictures that you've taken from magazines. That way there is often something new on his bulletin board for him to look at and ponder.

Later, as he is older, your child will enjoy putting up and taking down his own art work, rearranging his collection, and decorating his room by means of his bulletin board!

Chalkboard

Also, you might consider putting a chalkboard in your child's room or in a kitchen area, etc. The board should be as large as you can afford in terms of both space and cost. Mount the chalkboard at a level appropriate for your young child. A chalkboard is a lot like blocks in the sense that it stimulates use of the imagination, provides large and small motor exercise, and grows with your child without need of any monitoring on your part. One fat piece of chalk, an eraser and a large chalkboard provide endless possibilities for your child to create whatever he chooses. Important scribbles or beginning pictures will soon be gracing the board. Small fingers and hands will be hard at work, and large arm movements will produce exercise as well as designs. These movements are beneficial as "pre-writing" skills. Chalkboard activities grow with your child. Every week, he will increase in his ability to hold the chalk, and make it do more and more of what he wants. He will not quickly outgrow this form of play and have to wait for the purchase of a more "difficult" toy. Chalkboards, like blocks and boxes grow *with* your child for years to come!

Art then, is a means of expression, through song, dance, verse and prose, that releases feelings. Art emanates from the emotions and stirs the emotions in those who view it. Art is fun! Art is necessary! Provide frequent times of creative art for your child from an early age. Also, be sure to provide a wide variety of different avenues of art appreciation.

A Trip to the Art Gallery

For instance, a contemplative child can be taken at a very young age to galleries and museums. There, you can walk and quietly discuss one or two things that you especially notice. Find a large, colorful, interesting work of art and just stand or sit in front of it for a while. You do not need to explain it. Just soak in the color, texture and pattern, etc. Your child may just look with you and be very quiet. But, if he has things to say about the art work, listen to what he says. What does he like or dislike? In what types of things does he show interest? You will get to know him better through times like these as you listen to *who* he is.

Even though the length of time spent at a gallery or museum doesn't have to be very long, some children are still not yet ready for this type of activity. A good way to stimulate your active child's interest in art is to find large, colorful prints of famous artists and put them in your home or in his room. Obviously, museum-loving children will enjoy having special prints in their rooms also.

A Gallery at Home

You can find these kinds of pictures at a print or frame shop (many have catalogs from which you can order) and at various art galleries and museums. Though there are many wonderful works of art, some you might like to consider are:

Picasso's *Girl Holding a Dove*
Renoir's *The Umbrellas*, and *Lady With a Parasol*
Matisse's *Goldfish, Interior with Violin, Tree Near
    Trivaux Pond*, and *Harmony in Red*
Van Gogh's *Starry Night*, and *Gauguin's
    Armchair*
Monet's *La Grenouillere, Terrace at Sainte-
    Adresse, Women in the Garden*, and *Water
    Lillies*
Gauguin's *Still Life with Three Puppies*

(This list does not even brush the surface of all the wonderful famous paintings that might be chosen for a child's room. There are also many beautiful, imaginative paintings at art fairs done by local artists. These types of community art fairs often provide the opportunity to acquire original art at a very reasonable price. Many fine toy stores also offer prints rendered from famous children's stories such as Beatrix Potter's prints, Sheperd's prints from *Winnie the Pooh*, and other stories including *Goodnight Moon*.)

Looking at pictures by famous artists and enjoying good pictures in books is a great activity for that quiet time of the day. Try to slow down and provide times for reflecting, thinking and enjoying fine art, stories and music for at least a few minutes each day. (This is a habit that will benefit your entire family.)

The Literary Arts
(Prose, Poetry, Plays)

Choosing Good Books

With so many books available, it is sometimes difficult to find books that you believe should be part of your child's collection. You want to find books that have the special quality that makes them worth reading over and over—books that will become favorites. One way to help find good books is to read a book like *Honey for a Child's Heart* by Gladys Hunt, 1989 Zondervan, ISBN 0310263816. *Honey for a Child's Heart* examines the value of books and reading with your children, citing wonderful examples from family life. In her book, Hunt has included a reading list with well-loved titles. There are other volumes on good books by other editors, but perhaps the best way to locate good books is to find someone who knows and loves books and shares your values. Find out what *they* enjoy, and try these books.

Book Illustrations

In addition to looking for great story content, you will also want to find books that have exceptional art. Enjoy these wonderful books together with your child. Many of the "classic" books come in more than one edition. One edition may have plain or unimaginative illustrations while another edition of the same story has the most beautiful illustrations. Therefore, you will want to spend some time searching for books that not only inspire with their words but also with their illustrations!

Children's Poetry

Poetry is a must for early childhood. Poetry is *sound*. Poetry is *emotion*. Poetry is *fun*! Gyo Fujikawa's delightful illustrations make *A Child's Book of Poems*, published by Grosset and Dunlap, a volume which you and your child will greatly enjoy. Also try *A Child's Garden of Verse,* by Robert Louis Stevenson, and *The World of Christopher Robin*, by A. A. Milne, E. P. Dutton Publishers. Your child will be enriched when you read poetry to him. His discernment of sound, his knowledge of rhythm and rhyme, and his ability to appreciate and create poetic thoughts will grow as you read him lots of poetry. Your child will also experience many different emotions from the readings, and grow in his ability to express his own feelings.

The Performing Arts (Music, Dance and Drama)

Listen to different kinds of music at naptime. If you have the opportunity, you might want to attend a short children's concert. Or better yet, if you know some musicians (whether guitar and banjo, or piano and cello, etc.) invite them to play together for your young child and his friends. Then make them dinner! Decorate with a musical theme. Your child will remember this special musical evening!

Scenes From Childhood

There is also a wonderful piece of concert-style music called *Kinderscene* or *Scenes From Childhood* by Schumann. In this work, the composer has written thirteen musical sketches of childhood. The music will remind you of his sketch titles. Find a good quality recording of this musical piece and play it for several days. Then play just one part and ask your older child if the music reminds him of something. If he doesn't come up with an idea, share with him the theme (based on the sketch titles) for that part of the work. Each of the thirteen parts portrays a different aspect of early childhood. One segment is reminiscent of a child on a rocking horse. Another part sounds like children running up the stairs, etc. Talk with your child about the music and how it makes him feel. Ask him if he can imagine such a scene.

This type of activity will add to his appreciation and enjoyment of music as he continues to hear other compositions. He will probably begin to make up his own scenes and pictures for the music that he hears. The part of Schumann's musical childhood *Scenes* titled "Dreaming" is a great piece to play at bedtime. *Scenes from Childhood* is an enjoyable way to introduce classical music to your young child and have some interesting dialogue in the process. And, you can certainly continue to play different kinds of music, including concert-style, in your home from time to time.

Homemade Instruments

Another way to introduce music in your family is to make your own musical instruments. There are so many different kinds. You can make them carefully with love, and present them to your child whenever you are ready to make some music. With care they will last a lifetime. Or an older sibling can take part in the instrument making. This helps him feel productive and builds strong sibling ties—"My sister (or brother) made this drum for me!!"

You can make drums, colorful maracas, castanets, wood blocks, sand blocks, rhythm sticks, bells, etc. Look for books at your library and in your bookstore that show you how to create musical instruments. Homemade instruments can run the gamut from lovingly constructed heirlooms to simple, inexpensive instruments made from free materials recovered from the trash can! You might begin with a book called *Music Crafts for Kids (The How to Book of Music Discovery)*. It is written by Noel Fiarotta and Phyllis Fiarotta, 1993, Sterling Publishing, ISBN 0806904062. There are many easy types of instruments to make. If you can find this book, let it be a starting place for your musical discoveries and continue to explore your local library under "Musical instruments—Construction—Juvenile."

Making Music

If your family has other, older musicians, have them play some music. Let your young child use his instruments to keep the beat. He may want to *clap* the rhythm first with his hands. Try to keep such play from becoming a drill or teaching session. Let him enjoy the music and learn to hear the beat. Or, you can play music on a tape or CD player. Use music of different tempos. Listen to the beat. Clap or stamp to it and then use your instruments to keep the rhythm and the beat. Remember—this is a playtime! Eventually, your child will even learn to keep the beat to complex, syncopated melodies. For your very young child, try the "Wee Sing" cassette tape *Baby Band*, ISBN 0843139854, at your large local bookstore.

Learning to See Through Children's Eyes

This section is for *parents only*. These are book selections that will help you as a parent to see life from the vulnerable vantage point of a child. You *may* want to share them with your child someday. But, for now they are *your* reading, *your* homework in the ongoing process of becoming an understanding parent.

First, let's listen to some true stories of misunderstandings.

A mother and her young son were driving to the store. Her son said, "Mom, I'm going to teach Dad how to chew gum."
She said, "Son, your father knows how to chew gum."
"No, I don't think so," the son replied.
"Yes dear," she said, "he certainly knows how to chew gum. He just doesn't care for it. He doesn't like to chew gum."
"No Mom, I know he doesn't know how to chew gum. He told me so."
(Mother thinking quickly.) "Son, what *exactly* did your father say to you that makes you think he doesn't know how to chew gum?"
Her son replied, "Dad said, 'Michael, I don't know how you and your mother chew that gum!'"

A country family set a mouse trap one night. Then they put their son to bed and went to bed themselves. In just a few minutes the trap snapped and everyone heard it. The parents got up and the boy wanted to see the mouse, too. They let him, then put him back to bed and reset the trap. A few minutes later the trap snapped a second time. Again, the little boy wanted to see. The parents agreed, let him see the mouse, and put him back to bed. They reset the trap and it quickly went off for the third time.
The father exclaimed, "A triple header!"
The little boy wanted to see.
The parents said, "No, it's time to go to sleep."
The little boy began to cry. The cry turned to a wail. (Spoiled behavior you might think.) Since the child did not normally act like that, the parents went to talk to him. "I wanted to see the mouse," he cried.
"But you've already seen two," they said.
"Yes," the little boy answered, "but I've never seen one with three heads!"

Once, at his grandfather's funeral, a toddler was greeted by a relative and told, "My, you have your grandfather's nose!" Later, after the casket was buried, the little boy burst into tears. He seemed extremely upset, nearly frantic. His mother asked him what was wrong and with some careful questioning was able to find out. The little boy finally said, "I didn't want them to bury grampa without his nose!"

In each of these situations, the parents could have been hasty, thinking that their child was just "behaving badly" or just "being stubborn." The woman in the gum episode could have told her son he was being silly. You know, the "don't be ridiculous," line. Or she could have just let the silly conversation drop. The country parents could have let their son cry himself to sleep, perhaps always thinking that he'd missed the only three-headed mouse on the planet. And the parents at the funeral could have tried to comfort their child without ever really paying enough attention to discover the actual cause of the boy's distress.

Yet, in each of these cases, the parents tried to listen (*really* listen) to what their child was saying. Their reward for the extra "detective" work was a warm relationship created by clear communication and understanding. To a child, being able to communicate ideas, worries, and desires and having someone take the time to understand him means he is loved and accepted. After all, isn't that what parents want for their children? All it takes is valuable time.

Books to Help You Understand

The following books are children's stories, but they were selected for *you*, the parent, to read. You may or may not decide to share these books with your child *someday*. But for now, when you read these stories for yourself, you will get a glimpse into the world from a *child's point of view*. These stories will remind you of feelings and desires that you once had, but may have since forgotten. You will remember times of being misunderstood, or times when you could not get your parents to understand what it was you needed. And, you will remember how hard you tried to do things well and how often the results were less than you had hoped for. So, read these books with an understanding heart and you will find ways to apply what you learn in your own home.

Albert's Toothache, by Barbara Williams, 1988, E. P. Dutton, ISBN 0525253688. (In this story, Albert's mother "worries" too much. Albert's grandmother has the poignant line of the story which saves the day!)

Christina Katerina and the Box by Patricia Lee Gauch, Coward-McCann & Geoghegan, Inc. (You may feel that Christina is a bit demanding, but her mother is amazed at how many things Christina can make using only one box!)

Andrew Henry's Meadow by Doris Burn, Coward-McCann. (Andrew Henry is full of ideas. His parent's job is to find a creative outlet, rather than brush him aside.)

Little Bear by Else Homelund Minarik, 1957 Harper and Row, Publishers, ISBN 0064400044 (Little Bear knows how to pretend, and mother bear is wonderful at pretending along!)

Ramona the Brave, by Beverly Cleary, Dail-Yearling Publishers. (Ramona isn't always a model child, but often, when she's trying to be "so good," life seems to backfire. Any of the Ramona books will bring back memories and maybe even a few tears as you remember how difficult childhood can sometimes be.)

In addition to these helpful children's books, there are of course several adult titles that will help you as you seek wisdom and understanding in child-rearing. These books will touch your heart and give you inspiration in raising your children and in making a "home."

For the Children's Sake, Foundations of Education for Home and School, Susan Schaeffer Macaulay, 1984, Crossway Books, ISBN 089107290X

Honey for a Child's Heart, Gladys Hunt, 1989, Zondervan Publishing House, ISBN 0310263816

The Hidden Art of Homemaking, Edith Schaeffer, 1985, Tyndale House Publishing, ISBN 0842313982

What Is a Family?, Edith Schaeffer, 1993, Baker Book House, ISBN 0801083656

Additional Books and Tapes

Oh, What a Busy Day! by Gyo Fujikawa. Check your library for availability. (A pictorial account of the "busy-ness" of children in all its action and color. You can spend hours of enjoyment just looking at this book!)

A Time to Keep, by Tasha Tudor. (A look back at the childhoods of yesteryear. *Lots* of activity, packed into a month-by-month, seasonal format. A great way to subtly introduce the seasons and find more great activity ideas. Don't miss this one. You will be amazed!)

Our Animal Friends by Alice and Martin Provensen, 1974, Random House, Inc., New York, ISBN 0394821238. (Absolutely delightful!)

The Bible in Pictures for Little Eyes, Toddler Edition, 1997 by Tyndale House Publishers. (This has been a favorite for more than forty years.)

Read Aloud Bible Stories (Four Volumes) Volume 1, Ella K. Lindvall, 1982, Moody Press, Inc., ISBN 0802471633. (This wonderful book has large illustrations showing Bible characters, often from unusual and memorable points of view!)

Everybody Can Know, Francis and Edith Schaffer, 1975, Tyndale House Publishing, ISBN 0842307869. (A vehicle for sharing Bible stories with your family and friends and as an ongoing "way of life.")

Wee Sing Cassette Tapes

Baby Band ISBN 0843139854
Nursery Rhymes and Lullabies
ISBN 0843137940
America, Patriots and Pioneers
ISBN 0843137991
Children's Songs and Fingerplays
ISBN 0843137932
Fun and Folk
ISBN 0843138025
Sing Alongs
ISBN 0843138041
Bible Songs
ISBN 0843137991. (All your old favorites including such songs as "This Little Light of Mine," etc.)

In the end...

In the end, being together and having fun is what is really important. So go out and fly a kite on a windy day, have a picnic on a warm day, or play with your child on a rainy day (not during lightning storms!). Sail paper, aluminum or wooden boats in the puddles or the rivulets that flow down the street. Jump in the puddles. Who can make a bigger splash? Laugh and sing. Taste the rain. Take pans outside and let the showers fill them up. Recite the poem "Happiness" by A. A. Milne that begins, "John had Great Big Waterproof Boots on; John had a Great Big Waterproof Hat..." and when you've ended your play say, "Rain, rain, go away, Come again some other day...." Then, finish your playtime with a warm bath, soft towel and a good story like *Mrs. Duck's Lovely Day,* Vivienne Blake, l955, Rand McNally & Co. (Not in print at this time. Try your library.) All in all, it will have been a nice day for ducks, *and* for your family!

Remember, there is great treasure to be found and cherished in these shared experiences. A. A. Milne wrote a poem called "Come Out With Me" in which the young person makes a number of exciting observations. The child wants to share them with the adults in his life, but he is having difficulty getting anyone to give him some time. One of the lines of this poem poses a good question: *"All of them say 'Run along! I'm busy as can be...Run along! There's a little darling!' If I'm a little darling, why don't they come and see?"*

The stories and activities included in *Before Five in a Row* are carefully chosen so that your child *will have* plenty of time to spend with you. Time to grow, and laugh, and love. Time for you to listen to him and be understanding. Plenty of time for you to help color his childhood years golden!

Thank you for using *Before Five in a Row*. If you have enjoyed it, please tell a friend.

Jane Claire Lambert
April, 1997

Master Index

A

acting out 8, 26
alphabet 46
alphabet bath 121
"America the Beautiful" 10
animal babies 23
animals, caring for their babies 88
apron making 89
Arnosky, Jim 24
art gallery, trip 138
art materials 119
art projects 8, 11, 13, 18, 24, 26, 27, 32, 33, 61, 98, 134, 137
arts 134

B

avoiding messies 135
balance 66,
balance, posture 54
balancing 114
ball, bouncing 117
ball, catching 116
ball, dribbling 117
ball, playing 116
ball, rolling 116
balloons 117
balls 133
bath 11
bath, alphabet 121
bath time 121
beach 14
bear 28, 31
birthdays 26
blessings 73
blocks 128
boats 19
book illustrations 140
books, choosing good 139
books, comparing 19
books to help you understand 143
books, wordless 106

boxes 131, 132
bread 73
bubbles 117, 121
building 130
bulletin boards 138
bus 38
buttercup-dandelion game 67
butterflies 11

C

captain 19
care giving 58
caves 84, 85
chalkboards 138
Childcraft Encyclopedia 131
children's poetry 140
choosing good books 139
cities 89
classification 30, 31, 39, 41, 45, 70, 83, 87, 98, 102
clay 120, 136
clothesbag, making 10
clothing combinations 8
collage 61
color, creating with 8
color matching 21, 22
colors 8, 13, 18, 21, 22, 27, 33, 66, 82
colors, primary 34
compartmental organization 118
composition, musical 92, 93
comprehension 92
construction paper 13
contentment 74
cooking 123
coordination 114
costumes, storage 112
counting 46, 53, 67, 89, 90, 99
crab walk 114
crayons 13, 21, 22, 27
curiosity 81
cutting 120, 123, 135

D

dancing 110
dandelion-buttercup game 67

decisions, making 102
determination 57
dew 70
dog safety 83
dogs 83
dough, modeling 120, 136
Dr. Seuss 4
dragging 115
drama 91, 111

E

ear 67
emotions 69, 71
environment 78
escalator 98

F

fairy tales 34
families 92
family traditions 7
fears 50, 74
feather 77
fingerpainting 137
fish 15
five senses 78
flag, American 10
floating toys 121
flowers 11
food 10
"For the Beauty of the Earth" 72
frustration 54
Fujikawa, Gyo 140

G

gallery, home 139
galloping 115
game 99
games, hand 108
gardening 59
gardens 10, 11
geography 74
gratitude 89
grocery store scavenger hunt 126

scavenger hunt, grocery store 126
Scenes From Childhood 140
Schumann 140
scissors 135
sculpture 135
sculpture, wooden 75
search 92
searching games 9, 10, 11, 14, 68
seasons 62
seeds 58
senses, five 78
sequencing 15
shadows 49
shapes 11, 35, 39, 42, 123
shells 78
shopping list bingo 126
siblings 6, 8, 9
silhouette 82
similarities and differences 75
singing 51, 109
skipping 115
small motor control 118
snow 62
snowy day 9
soap paints 121
song 28, 32
sorting games 118
sounds, loud 68
sounds, soft 68
stamping projects 137
Starry Night 19
stars 11, 20, 33, 76
Stevenson, Robert Louis 8, 50, 140
stirring 123
store, playing 125, 131
stores 38
storing your costumes 112
storms 15
storytelling 34, 37
sun 33
surprise ball making 13, 133

T
talking and listening 106
theatre, puppet 113

thinking place 25
"This is My Father's World" 72
threading 119
toys 127
toys, floating 121
toys, selection 127
toys, story character 22
tracking 18
tracks 62, 79
trees 89
trip to art gallery 138
trip to the theatre 113
tumbling 114

U
unbirthdays 26

V
vacations 101
Van Gogh 19
videotaping 113
viewpoint, art 24
visual arts 134
vocabulary 18, 24

W
washcloth game 121
watercolor 61
weather 45, 62, 102
wedge 82
Wee Sing tapes 11, 109, 141, 145
weights 125
whales 19
Wilkin, Eloise 9, 35
wooden blocks 128
wordless books 106
words, coining new 24
wrestling 114

Y
"Yankee Doodle" 10

Z
zoology 39

Other Products from Five in a Row

Before Five in a Row by Jane Claire Lambert- This treasury of learning ideas was created for children ages 2-4. Enjoy exploring 24 wonderful children's books while building a warm and solid foundation for the learning years just around the corner. ISBN 1-888659-04-1 $24.95

Five in a Row Volume 1 by Jane Claire Lambert- Volume 1 contains 19 unit studies built around 19 of the very best children's books ever printed. Each unit takes five days to complete. Created primarily for children ages 4-8 but don't be afraid to include other ages too! ISBN 1-888659-00-9 $19.95

Five in a Row Volume 2 by Jane Claire Lambert- Volume 2 explores 21 more outstanding children's books. Each unit takes five days to complete. Created for ages 4-8. ISBN 1-888659-01-7 $24.95

Five in a Row Volume 3 by Jane Claire Lambert- Volume 3 explores 15 additional outstanding children's books. Each unit takes five days to complete. Created for ages 4-8. ISBN 1-888659-02-5 $19.95

Five in a Row Christian Character and Bible Study Supplement by Jane Claire Lambert- This wonderful resource teaches hundreds of non-denominational Bible lessons and concepts using the first *three* volumes of *Five in a Row*. Teach your children about obeying parents, kindness, generosity, good stewardship, forgiveness and more. Ages 4-8. ISBN 1-888659-03-3 $17.95

Laminated Full Color Story Disks by Jane Claire Lambert- Each volume of *Five in a Row* contains black and white *story disks*. Use these little half-dollar sized drawings to teach children geography by attaching them to your own large, world map as you explore each new *Five in a Row* story. Just cut out the disks, color and laminate them. *However*, we offer this *optional* set of already colored, laminated disks for those who prefer to save the time needed to prepare their own. These disks are printed in full color and heat laminated—ready to use. One set of these disks covers all *three* volumes of *Five in a Row*. Beautiful and ready to enjoy! $15.00

The Five in a Row Cookbook by Becky Jane Lambert. This companion volume to *Five in a Row* (Volumes 1-3) and *Beyond Five in a Row* (Volumes 1-3) provides complete recipes and menus to complement each story you study. You'll enjoy the opportunity to wrap up each unit with a family meal, a time of celebration, and the opportunity for your students to share their achievements. You'll also appreciate the scrapbook area for photos, notes and homeschool memories. ISBN 1-888659-11-4 $22.95

Beyond Five in a Row Volume 1 by Becky Jane Lambert- Here is the answer for all those moms who have asked, "What do I do after *Five in a Row?*" You'll find the same creative, thought-provoking activities and lesson ideas you've come to expect from *Five in a Row* using outstanding chapter books for older children. Volume 1 will keep your students busy for many months with history, geography, science, language arts, fine arts and issues of human relationships. Each unit also includes numerous discussion questions, career path investigations and much more. Volume 1 requires *The Boxcar Children, Homer Price*, and the *Childhood of Famous American Series* biographies of *Thomas A. Edison- Young Inventor* and *Betsy Ross- Designer of Our Flag*. Created for ages 8-12. ISBN 1-888659-13-0 $24.95

Beyond Five in a Row Volume 2 by Becky Jane Lambert. Requires *Sarah Plain and Tall, The Story of George Washington Carver, Skylark,* and *Helen Keller.* ISBN 1-888659-14-9 $24.95

Beyond Five in a Row Volume 3 by Becky Jane Lambert. Requires *Neil Armstrong-Young Flyer, The Cricket in Times Square, Marie Curie- and the Discovery of Radium,* and *The Saturdays.* ISBN 1-888659-15-7 $24.95

Beyond Five in a Row Bible Christian Character and Bible Supplement by Becky Jane Lambert- This companion volume to *Beyond Five in a Row* provides a rich selection of the wonderful Bible references and strong character lessons you've come to expect from *Five in a Row*. This valuable supplement teaches traditional Christian values such as honoring parents, forgiveness, generosity, etc. Covers all three volumes of *Beyond Five in a Row* in one handy volume. Effective and easy to use! ISBN 1-888659-16-5 $17.95

Above & Beyond Five in a Row *The First Adventure* by Becky Jane Lambert. This latest offering from Five in a Row Publishing is based on Rachel Field's Newbery award winning book *"Hitty: Her First Hundred Years."* This stand-alone unit study is aimed at students ages 12-14 years of age and includes a wide variety of learning opportunities in the best *Five in a Row* tradition. Each "adventure" will take several months to complete. ISBN 1-888659-17-3 $19.95

Five in a Row Holiday: *Through the Seasons* by Jane Claire Lambert and Becky Jane Lambert *Five in a Row Holiday* is by far our most personal, intimate book, sharing our own family's values, traditions and memories in a way that we hope will inspire you to take whatever seems good to you from our experience and combine it with your family's unique traditions as you create your own family holiday heritage. Filled with individual holiday unit studies, activities, recipes, projects and memories, this book is more than just curriculum. You'll discover a delightful treasury of holiday enjoyment.
ISBN 1-888659-12-2 $24.95

* IMPORTANT - Please be sure to include your street address for UPS shipping. They cannot deliver to a Post Office Box!

Name _____

Address * _____

City/State/Zip _____ Phone _____

Item	Qty.	Price Ea.	Total
Five in a Row Holiday-through the seasons		$24.95	
Before Five in a Row Ages 2-4		$24.95	
Five in a Row Cookbook		$22.95	
Five in a Row-Volume 1 Ages 4-8	pkg	$19.95	
Five in a Row-Volume 2 Ages 4-8	pkg	$24.95	
Five in a Row-Volume 3 Ages 4-8	pkg	$19.95	
Five in a Row Bible Supplement	pkg	$17.95	
Laminated Full Color Story Disks	pkg	$15.00	
Five in a Row Cookbook	pkg	$22.95	
Complete FIAR Pkg. (Save 10%)		**$108.00**	
Beyond Five in a Row Vol. 1 Ages 8-12	pkg	$24.95	
Beyond Five in a Row Vol. 2 Ages 8-12	pkg	$24.95	
Beyond Five in a Row Vol. 3 Ages 8-12	pkg	$24.95	
Beyond Five in a Row Bible Supp. V.1-3	pkg	$ 17.95	
Five in a Row Cookbook	pkg	$22.95	
Complete BEYOND Pkg. (Save 10%)		**$104.00**	
NEW *Above & Beyond Five in a Row*		$19.95	
The First Adventure "Hitty" (ages 12-14)			
6-Cassette FIAR Conference Tape Set		$32.40	
4-Cassette Steve Lambert Tape Set		$21.60	
Five in a Row Book Tote		$12.95	
Reading Made Easy Phonics		$45.00	
by Valerie Bendt			
Merchandise Total			
Shipping Charges*		$5.95	
MO Residents add 7.10% Tax			
Order Total			

Make Check Payable To:
Five in a Row
P.O. Box 707
Grandview, MO
64030-0707

Thank you for ordering *Five in a Row*

Other Products from Five in a Row

Before Five in a Row by Jane Claire Lambert- This treasury of learning ideas was created for children ages 2-4. Enjoy exploring 24 wonderful children's books while building a warm and solid foundation for the learning years just around the corner. ISBN 1-888659-04-1 $24.95

Five in a Row *Volume 1* by Jane Claire Lambert- Volume 1 contains 19 unit studies built around 19 of the very best children's books ever printed. Each unit takes five days to complete. Created primarily for children ages 4-8 but don't be afraid to include other ages too! ISBN 1-888659-00-9 $19.95

Five in a Row *Volume 2* by Jane Claire Lambert- Volume 2 explores 21 more outstanding children's books. Each unit takes five days to complete. Created for ages 4-8. ISBN 1-888659-01-7 $24.95

Five in a Row *Volume 3* by Jane Claire Lambert- Volume 3 explores 15 additional outstanding children's books. Each unit takes five days to complete. Created for ages 4-8. ISBN 1-888659-02-5 $19.95

Five in a Row Christian Character and Bible Study Supplement by Jane Claire Lambert- This wonderful resource teaches hundreds of non-denominational Bible lessons and concepts using the first *three* volumes of *Five in a Row*. Teach your children about obeying parents, kindness, generosity, good stewardship, forgiveness and more. Ages 4-8. ISBN 1-888659-03-3 $17.95

Laminated Full Color Story Disks by Jane Claire Lambert- Each volume of *Five in a Row* contains black and white *story disks*. Use these little half-dollar sized drawings to teach children geography by attaching them to your own large, world map as you explore each new *Five in a Row* story. Just cut out the disks, color and laminate them. *However*, we offer this *optional* set of already colored, laminated disks for those who prefer to save the time needed to prepare their own. These disks are printed in full color and heat laminated—ready to use. One set of these disks covers all *three* volumes of *Five in a Row*. Beautiful and ready to enjoy! $15.00

The Five in a Row Cookbook by Becky Jane Lambert. This companion volume to *Five in a Row* (Volumes 1-3) and *Beyond Five in a Row* (Volumes 1-3) provides complete recipes and menus to complement each story you study. You'll enjoy the opportunity to wrap up each unit with a family meal, a time of celebration, and the opportunity for your students to share their achievements. You'll also appreciate the scrapbook area for photos, notes and homeschool memories. ISBN 1-888659-11-4 $22.95

Beyond Five in a Row *Volume 1* by Becky Jane Lambert- Here is the answer for all those moms who have asked, "What do I do after *Five in a Row?*" You'll find the same creative, thought-provoking activities and lesson ideas you've come to expect from *Five in a Row* using outstanding chapter books for older children. Volume 1 will keep your students busy for many months with history, geography, science, language arts, fine arts and issues of human relationships. Each unit also includes numerous discussion questions, career path investigations and much more. Volume 1 requires *The Boxcar Children, Homer Price,* and the *Childhood of Famous American Series* biographies of *Thomas A. Edison- Young Inventor and Betsy Ross- Designer of Our Flag.* Created for ages 8-12. ISBN 1-888659-13-0 $24.95

Beyond Five in a Row *Volume 2* by Becky Jane Lambert. Requires *Sarah Plain and Tall, The Story of George Washington Carver, Skylark,* and *Helen Keller.* ISBN 1-888659-14-9 $24.95

Beyond Five in a Row *Volume 3* by Becky Jane Lambert. Requires *Neil Armstrong-Young Flyer, The Cricket in Times Square, Marie Curie- and the Discovery of Radium,* and *The Saturdays.* ISBN 1-888659-15-7 $24.95

Beyond Five in a Row Bible Christian Character and Bible Supplement by Becky Jane Lambert- This companion volume to *Beyond Five in a Row* provides a rich selection of the wonderful Bible references and strong character lessons you've come to expect from *Five in a Row*. This valuable supplement teaches traditional Christian values such as honoring parents, forgiveness, generosity, etc. Covers all three volumes of *Beyond Five in a Row* in one handy volume. Effective and easy to use! ISBN 1-888659-16-5 $17.95

Above & Beyond Five in a Row *The First Adventure* by Becky Jane Lambert. This latest offering from Five in a Row Publishing is based on Rachel Field's Newbery award winning book *"Hitty: Her First Hundred Years."* This stand-alone unit study is aimed at students ages 12-14 years of age and includes a wide variety of learning opportunities in the best *Five in a Row* tradition. Each "adventure" will take several months to complete. ISBN 1-888659-17-3 $19.95

Five in a Row Holiday: *Through the Seasons* by Jane Claire Lambert and Becky Jane Lambert *Five in a Row Holiday* is by far our most personal, intimate book, sharing our own family's values, traditions and memories in a way that we hope will inspire you to take whatever seems good to you from our experience and combine it with your family's unique traditions as you create your own family holiday heritage. Filled with individual holiday unit studies, activities, recipes, projects and memories, this book is more than just curriculum. You'll discover a delightful treasury of holiday enjoyment. ISBN 1-888659-12-2 $24.95

Name _____

Address * _____

City/State/Zip _____   Phone _____

Item	Qty.	Price Ea.	Total
Five in a Row Holiday-through the seasons		$24.95	
Before Five in a Row Ages 2-4		$24.95	
Five in a Row Cookbook		$22.95	
Five in a Row-Volume 1 Ages 4-8	pkg	$19.95	
Five in a Row-Volume 2 Ages 4-8	pkg	$24.95	
Five in a Row-Volume 3 Ages 4-8	pkg	$19.95	
Five in a Row Bible Supplement	pkg	$17.95	
Laminated Full Color Story Disks	pkg	$15.00	
Five in a Row Cookbook	pkg	$22.95	
Complete FIAR Pkg. (Save 10%)		**$108.00**	
Beyond Five in a Row Vol. 1 Ages 8-12	pkg	$24.95	
Beyond Five in a Row Vol. 2 Ages 8-12	pkg	$24.95	
Beyond Five in a Row Vol. 3 Ages 8-12	pkg	$24.95	
Beyond Five in a Row Bible Supp. V.1-3	pkg	$ 17.95	
Five in a Row Cookbook	pkg	$22.95	
Complete BEYOND Pkg. (Save 10%)		**$104.00**	
NEW Above & Beyond Five in a Row*		$19.95	
The First Adventure "Hitty" (ages 12-14)			
6-Cassette FIAR Conference Tape Set		$32.40	
4-Cassette Steve Lambert Tape Set		$21.60	
Five in a Row Book Tote		$12.95	
Reading Made Easy Phonics		$45.00	
by Valerie Bendt			
		Merchandise Total	
		Shipping Charges*	$5.95
		MO Residents add 7.10% Tax	
		Order Total	

Make Check Payable To:

Five in a Row
P.O. Box 707
Grandview, MO
64030-0707

Thank you for ordering *Five in a Row*

Other Products from Five in a Row

Before Five in a Row by Jane Claire Lambert- This treasury of learning ideas was created for children ages 2-4. Enjoy exploring 24 wonderful children's books while building a warm and solid foundation for the learning years just around the corner. ISBN 1-888659-04-1 $24.95

Five in a Row *Volume 1* by Jane Claire Lambert- Volume 1 contains 19 unit studies built around 19 of the very best children's books ever printed. Each unit takes five days to complete. Created primarily for children ages 4-8 but don't be afraid to include other ages too! ISBN 1-888659-00-9 $19.95

Five in a Row *Volume 2* by Jane Claire Lambert- Volume 2 explores 21 more outstanding children's books. Each unit takes five days to complete. Created for ages 4-8. ISBN 1-888659-01-7 $24.95

Five in a Row *Volume 3* by Jane Claire Lambert- Volume 3 explores 15 additional outstanding children's books. Each unit takes five days to complete. Created for ages 4-8. ISBN 1-888659-02-5 $19.95

Five in a Row Christian Character and Bible Study Supplement by Jane Claire Lambert- This wonderful resource teaches hundreds of non-denominational Bible lessons and concepts using the first *three* volumes of *Five in a Row*. Teach your children about obeying parents, kindness, generosity, good stewardship, forgiveness and more. Ages 4-8. ISBN 1-888659-03-3 $17.95

Laminated Full Color Story Disks by Jane Claire Lambert- Each volume of *Five in a Row* contains black and white *story disks*. Use these little half-dollar sized drawings to teach children geography by attaching them to your own large, world map as you explore each new *Five in a Row* story. Just cut out the disks, color and laminate them. *However*, we offer this *optional* set of already colored, laminated disks for those who prefer to save the time needed to prepare their own. These disks are printed in full color and heat laminated—ready to use. One set of these disks covers all *three* volumes of *Five in a Row*. Beautiful and ready to enjoy! $15.00

The Five in a Row Cookbook by Becky Jane Lambert. This companion volume to *Five in a Row* (Volumes 1-3) and *Beyond Five in a Row* (Volumes 1-3) provides complete recipes and menus to complement each story you study. You'll enjoy the opportunity to wrap up each unit with a family meal, a time of celebration, and the opportunity for your students to share their achievements. You'll also appreciate the scrapbook area for photos, notes and homeschool memories. ISBN 1-888659-11-4 $22.95

Beyond Five in a Row *Volume 1* by Becky Jane Lambert- Here is the answer for all those moms who have asked, "What do I do *after Five in a Row*?" You'll find the same creative, thought-provoking activities and lesson ideas you've come to expect from *Five in a Row* using outstanding chapter books for older children. Volume 1 will keep your students busy for many months with history, geography, science, language arts, fine arts and issues of human relationships. Each unit also includes numerous discussion questions, career path investigations and much more. Volume 1 requires *The Boxcar Children, Homer Price,* and the *Childhood of Famous American Series* biographies of *Thomas A. Edison- Young Inventor* and *Betsy Ross- Designer of Our Flag*. Created for ages 8-12. ISBN 1-888659-13-0 $24.95

Beyond Five in a Row *Volume 2* by Becky Jane Lambert. Requires *Sarah Plain and Tall, The Story of George Washington Carver, Skylark,* and *Helen Keller*. ISBN 1-888659-14-9 $24.95

Beyond Five in a Row *Volume 3* by Becky Jane Lambert. Requires *Neil Armstrong-Young Flyer, The Cricket in Times Square, Marie Curie- and the Discovery of Radium,* and *The Saturdays*. ISBN 1-888659-15-7 $24.95

Beyond Five in a Row Bible Christian Character and Bible Supplement by Becky Jane Lambert- This companion volume to *Beyond Five in a Row* provides a rich selection of the wonderful Bible references and strong character lessons you've come to expect from *Five in a Row*. This valuable supplement teaches traditional Christian values such as honoring parents, forgiveness, generosity, etc. Covers all three volumes of *Beyond Five in a Row* in one handy volume. Effective and easy to use! ISBN 1-888659-16-5 $17.95

Above & Beyond Five in a Row *The First Adventure* by Becky Jane Lambert. This latest offering from Five in a Row Publishing is based on Rachel Field's Newbery award winning book *"Hitty: Her First Hundred Years."* This stand-alone unit study is aimed at students ages 12-14 years of age and includes a wide variety of learning opportunities in the best *Five in a Row* tradition. Each "adventure" will take several months to complete. ISBN 1-888659-17-3 $19.95

Five in a Row Holiday: Through the Seasons by Jane Claire Lambert and Becky Jane Lambert *Five in a Row Holiday* is by far our most personal, intimate book, sharing our own family's values, traditions and memories in a way that we hope will inspire you to take whatever seems good to you from our experience and combine it with your family's unique traditions as you create your own family holiday heritage. Filled with individual holiday unit studies, activities, recipes, projects and memories, this book is more than just curriculum. You'll discover a delightful treasury of holiday enjoyment. ISBN 1-888659-12-2 $24.95

* IMPORTANT - Please be sure to include your street address for UPS shipping. They cannot deliver to a Post Office Box!

Name _____

Address * _____

City/State/Zip _____ Phone _____

Item	Qty.	Price Ea.	Total
Five in a Row Holiday-through the seasons		$24.95	
Before Five in a Row Ages 2-4		$24.95	
Five in a Row Cookbook		$22.95	
Five in a Row-Volume 1 Ages 4-8	pkg	$19.95	
Five in a Row-Volume 2 Ages 4-8	pkg	$24.95	
Five in a Row-Volume 3 Ages 4-8	pkg	$19.95	
Five in a Row Bible Supplement	pkg	$17.95	
Laminated Full Color Story Disks	pkg	$15.00	
Five in a Row Cookbook	pkg	$22.95	
Complete FIAR Pkg. (Save 10%)		**$108.00**	
Beyond Five in a Row Vol. 1 Ages 8-12	pkg	$24.95	
Beyond Five in a Row Vol. 2 Ages 8-12	pkg	$24.95	
Beyond Five in a Row Vol. 3 Ages 8-12	pkg	$24.95	
Beyond Five in a Row Bible Supp. V.1-3	pkg	$ 17.95	
Five in a Row Cookbook	pkg	$22.95	
Complete BEYOND Pkg. (Save 10%)		**$104.00**	
NEW Above & Beyond Five in a Row		$19.95	
The First Adventure "Hitty" **(ages 12-14)**			
6-Cassette FIAR Conference Tape Set		$32.40	
4-Cassette Steve Lambert Tape Set		$21.60	
Five in a Row Book Tote		$12.95	
Reading Made Easy Phonics		$45.00	
by Valerie Bendt			
		Merchandise Total	
		Shipping Charges*	$5.95
		MO Residents add 7.10% Tax	
		Order Total	

Make Check Payable To:

Five in a Row
P.O. Box 707
Grandview, MO
64030-0707

Thank you for ordering *Five in a Row*